ABORTION:

WHOSE RIGHT?

Institute of Ideas
Expanding the Boundaries of Public Debate

ABORTION:

WHOSE RIGHT?

Institute of Ideas
Expanding the Boundaries of Public Debate

Ellie Lee
Emily Jackson
Helen Watt
Theodore Darymple
Ann Furedi
Mary Kenny

Hodder & Stoughton
A MEMBER OF THE HODDER HEADLINE GROUP

DEBATING MATTERS

Orders: please contact Bookpoint Ltd, 130 Milton Park, Abingdon, Oxon OX14 4SB. Telephone: (44) 01235 827720. Fax: (44) 01235 400454. Lines are open from 9.00–6.00, Monday to Saturday, with a 24-hour message answering service. Email address: orders@bookpoint.co.uk

British Library Cataloguing in Publication Data
A catalogue record for this title is available from the British Library

ISBN 0 340 85736 6

First published 2002
Impression number   10 9 8 7 6 5 4 3 2 1
Year   2007 2006 2005 2004 2003 2002

Typeset by Transet Limited, Coventry, England
Printed in Great Britain for Hodder & Stoughton Educational, a division of Hodder Headline Plc, 338 Euston Road, London NW1 3BH by Cox & Wyman, Reading, Berks.

CONTENTS

PREFACE

Since the summer of 2000, the Institute of Ideas (IoI) has organized a wide range of live debates, conferences and salons on issues of the day. The success of these events indicates a thirst for intelligent debate that goes beyond the headline or the sound-bite. The IoI was delighted to be approached by Hodder & Stoughton, with a proposal for a set of books modelled on this kind of debate. The *Debating Matters* series is the result and reflects the Institute's commitment to opening up discussions on issues which are often talked about in the public realm, but rarely interrogated outside of academia, government committee or specialist milieu. Each book comprises a set of essays, which address one of four themes: law, science, society and the arts and media.

Our aim is to avoid approaching questions in too black and white a way. Instead, in each book, essayists will give voice to the various sides of the debate on contentious contemporary issues, in a readable style. Sometimes approaches will overlap, but from different perspectives, and some contributors may not take a 'for or against' stance, but simply present the evidence dispassionately.

Debating Matters dwells on key issues that have emerged as concerns over the last few years, but which represent more than short-lived fads. For example, anxieties about the problem of 'designer babies', discussed in one book in this series, have risen over the past decade. But further scientific developments in reproductive technology, accompanied by a widespread cultural distrust of the implications of these developments, means the debate about 'designer babies' is set to continue. Similarly, preoccupations with the weather may hit the news at times of flooding or extreme weather conditions, but the underlying concern about global warming and the idea that man's intervention into nature is causing the world harm, addressed in another book in the *Debating Matters* series, is an enduring theme in contemporary culture.

At the heart of the series is the recognition that in today's culture, debate is too frequently sidelined. So-called political correctness has ruled out too many issues as inappropriate for debate. The oft noted 'dumbing down' of culture and education has taken its toll on intelligent and challenging public discussion. In the House of Commons, and in politics more generally, exchanges of views are downgraded in favour of consensus and arguments over matters of principle are a rarity. In our universities, current relativist orthodoxy celebrates all views as equal, as though there are no arguments to win. Whatever the cause, many in academia bemoan the loss of the vibrant contestation and robust refutation of ideas in seminars, lecture halls and research papers. Trends in the media have led to more 'reality TV', than TV debates about real issues and newspapers favour the personal column rather than the extended polemical essay. All these trends and more have had a chilling effect on debate.

But for society in general, and for individuals within it, the need for a robust intellectual approach to major issues of our day is essential. The *Debating Matters* series is one contribution to encouraging contest about ideas, so vital if we are to understand the world and play a part in shaping its future. You may not agree with all the essays in the *Debating Matters* series and you may not find all your questions answered or all your intellectual curiosity sated, but we hope you will find the essays stimulating, thought provoking and a spur to carrying on the debate long after you have closed the book.

Claire Fox, Director, Institute of Ideas

NOTES ON THE CONTRIBUTORS

Dr Theodore Darymple qualified as a doctor in 1974 and has worked in Africa and the Pacific. He currently works as a doctor in an inner city hospital and a prison. He has written a column for *The Spectator* for 11 years and is contributing editor to the *City Journal of New York*. He has published *Mass Listeria: The Meaning of Health Scares* and *An Intelligent Person's Guide to Medicine*, and a novel, *So Little Done: The Testament of a Serial Killer*. His latest book is *View From the Bottom*.

Ann Furedi is former Director of Communications of the British Pregnancy Advisory Service, Britain's largest provider of specialist abortion care. Previously she was Executive Director of the family planning advocacy charity, Birth Control Trust. Furedi has been involved in advocacy on reproductive rights for almost 20 years. She has written extensively on related issues (including books on women's health and unplanned pregnancy) and taken part in various broadcast debates.

Emily Jackson is a senior lecturer in law at the London School of Economics. She previously taught at St Catharine's College, Cambridge and Birkbeck College, London. Her principal teaching and research interests are in the field of medical law, with particular emphasis on reproductive issues. In addition to a number of articles, she is the author of *Regulating Reproduction* (2001).

Mary Kenny is a well-established journalist and writer in Britain and Ireland. She is associated with the *Telegraph* and *Mail* newspapers in London, and the *Irish Independent* in Dublin. Her most recent book is a social history of Ireland during the twentieth century, *Goodbye the Catholic Ireland*, which is going into its third American printing in 2002. She is working on a historical biography to be published early in 2003.

Ellie Lee is a research fellow in the Department of Sociology and Social Policy at the University of Southampton. Her research interests concern the sociology of social problems, and policy developments in the areas of the regulation of reproductive technology and mental health. She is commissioning editor for the law section of the *Debating Matters* series.

Helen Watt is Director of the Linacre Centre for Healthcare Ethics, London. Prior to taking up this post in 2001, she held the position of Research Fellow at the Centre. From 1993 to 1996, she was also Senior Research Associate at Peterhouse, Cambridge. She holds a Ph.D. in Philosophy from the University of Edinburgh and an honors degree in Italian from the University of Western Australia. She is the author of *Life and Death in Healthcare Ethics: A short introduction* (2000).

INTRODUCTION
Ellie Lee

Most issues discussed in the *Debating Matters* series are currently the subject of intense public debate in Britain. The issue discussed in this book – abortion – is different in this respect. While abortion has made the news occasionally over the past few years (for example, where men have attempted to use the law to prevent their partners from terminating a pregnancy, or where a woman has had an 'unusual' kind of abortion, such as of one of twin fetuses) it is not regularly debated. Most significantly, perhaps, it is not an issue that is of political interest. British politicians and policy makers are not, visibly at least, engaged in debate on the abortion issue.

To the contrary, it has been apparent in recent years that abortion is not considered to be an issue that politicians should comment on. New Labour in particular has made it very clear that it does not want to be associated with holding a position on the issue. In 1996, in the run-up to the general election, Tony Blair stated in an interview with the *Daily Telegraph* that he strongly disagreed with attempts by anyone to turn abortion into a political issue, and that 'I intend to do everything in my power to keep abortion out of party politics'. According to Catherine Bennett, columnist for *The Guardian*, Janet Anderson, then spokeswoman on 'women's issues' for the Labour Party, indicated there would be 'virtual silence' from new Labour regarding the issue of women's need for abortion, when she refused to provide any comment on the issue – a silence that has continued since. The view that abortion should not be a matter for political debate seems to be shared by the Conservative Party leadership, which has swiftly contained attempts from within its ranks to encourage debate about abortion. Then Shadow Health Secretary, Liam Fox, did so in 2001. In the run-up to the general election that year, he argued that abortion should be an election issue, and that there 'should be a huge restriction if not abolition' of the current law. As Andrew Lansley, then Shadow Cabinet Office Minister, explained on the *Today* programme in response, however, the Conservative Party had no plans to make abortion an election issue, or to attempt to change the law. It seemed clear, from his obvious embarrassment about Fox's comments, that the last thing the Tory Party wanted was to become associated with holding a position on abortion.

The current consensus regarding the undesirability of political debate on abortion has emerged following a time when the issue was high profile in Parliament. Parliamentary debate about abortion was most prevalent during the 1970s and 1980s, and its impetus was sentiment opposed to increased access to abortion. There were 15 parliamentary bills between 1967 and 1989 attacking the 1967 Abortion Act that made abortion legally available in Britain. The main bills were introduced in 1974 (the White Bill), 1979 (the Corrie Bill) and 1987 (the Alton Bill). Others were introduced in 1977, 1978, 1985, 1986 and 1987 (there were three anti-abortion bills this year, other than the Alton Bill). This number of bills suggests that during this time there was significant sentiment in Parliament that believed it should be made more difficult for women to get abortions.

Yet none of these bills was passed – indeed, without exception, none reached the point where they were voted on. In fact, only once since 1967 has the abortion law been reformed in Parliament. This took place in 1990, through Section 37 of the Human Fertilisation and Embryology Act, an act that deals mainly with the regulation of embryo research and the provision of infertility treatment. (Another book in this series, *Designer Babies: Where Should We Draw The Line?* discusses this legislation in more detail.) In contrast with previous abortion bills, the Government allocated time for debate in 1990, in order to ensure an amendment was passed that would finally resolve the issue which had formed the main focus for debate through the 1980s – the question of the legal time-limit for abortion. In the end, after a very protracted debate and series of votes, the time-limit proposed by the Conservative MP Geoffrey Howe, that specified a limit of 24 weeks with exceptions where the life of the woman was at risk, or where there was 'substantial risk of serious abnormality' in the fetus, was accepted.

In practice the new amendment changed little. The number of abortions carried out after 24 weeks, for reasons other than fetal abnormality, was tiny. In 1989, the year before the Act was amended, only 22 were performed after 24 weeks, and of these 18 were for fetal abnormality, and four to save the woman's life. It had been the case since the 1967 Act was passed that the vast majority of abortions were performed in the first 14 weeks of pregnancy. The significance of the amendment, however, was that it signalled a clear consensus that an end should be put to debate about abortion. As Kenneth Clarke, then Secretary of State for Health, told the House of Commons, 'this is a suitable opportunity for the House to have a day at the end of which it can come to a conclusion, which should last a long time, on the time limits and future operation of the 1967 Act'. The main part of the Abortion Act 1967 (as amended) is as follows:

A person shall not be guilty of an offence under the law relating to abortion when a pregnancy is terminated by a registered medical practitioner if two registered medical practitioners are of the opinion formed in good faith –

(a) that the pregnancy has not exceeded its twenty-fourth week and that the continuance of the pregnancy would involve risk, greater than if the pregnancy were terminated, of injury to the physical or mental health of the pregnant woman or any existing children of her family; or

(b) that the termination is necessary to prevent grave permanent injury to the physical or mental health of the pregnant woman; or

(c) that the continuance of the pregnancy would involve risk to the life of the pregnant woman, greater than if the pregnancy were terminated; or

(d) that there is substantial risk that if the child were born it would suffer from such physical or mental abnormalities as to be seriously handicapped.

It is this piece of legislation, then, that has come to be accepted as beyond debate in Parliament. Its features, that underpin the discussion in the essays in this volume, are first, that it adds to, rather than replaces, the existing abortion law. As Emily Jackson discusses in more detail in her essay, abortion in Britain remains regulated by the 1861 Offences Against the Person Act. Under this statute:

Every woman, being with child, who, with intent to procure her own miscarriage, shall unlawfully administer to herself any poison or other noxious thing, or shall unlawfully use any instrument or other means whatsoever with like intent, and whosoever, with intent to procure the miscarriage of any woman whether she be or be not with child...shall be guilty of an offence, and being convicted thereof shall be liable to imprisonment.

Thus, in Britain, an offence is committed by the person who administers the 'poison' or uses an 'instrument' to 'procure a miscarriage', and by the woman herself, whether the woman concerned is actually pregnant or not. The 1967 Abortion Act does not decriminalize abortion. Rather, it creates a defence against the illegality of abortion established under the 1861 Act, by allowing an abortion to be performed if two doctors agree 'in good faith' that it is necessary. The second key feature of British abortion law, therefore, is that abortion is deemed legal not on the grounds that a pregnant woman has a right to it, but where medical opinion believes it can be performed, in accordance with one of the four medical grounds stated above.

It is perhaps not difficult to see why this form of law has proved so durable, and why politicians have resisted attempts to reform it substantially. Since the statute deems neither fetuses nor women the bearers of rights, but rather presents abortion as a medical issue to be decided on by doctors, it circumvents the controversial issue of the morality of abortion. To put it another way, the legality of abortion in Britain is not decided by making a judgement about whether fetuses, or women, have interests at stake that should be protected by the law. Rather its legality rests on whether it is deemed medically necessary to protect the health of a woman or members of her existing family through allowing a woman to terminate a pregnancy. As a result, abortion is placed beyond moral conflict about whether the rights of fetuses, or women, matter most. It may be for this reason that, in Britain, abortion has not become subject to the kind of heated debate and political contest where such interests are given legal protection as, for example, in the United States of America, where the right of a woman to end a pregnancy is legally protected, or Ireland, where the right to life of the unborn child is enshrined in the law. British politicians are likely to be glad they can thus avoid being drawn into such fraught debate.

The fact that abortion law has ceased to be a focus for political debate and contest in Britain does not mean, however, that it ceases to be a subject of interest. To the contrary, beyond the arena of debate in Parliament, there are significant developments that have taken place, for example, in the provision of abortion in practice, and it is these that form the starting point for the essays in this book. Most notably, whilst on paper the 1967 Abortion Act (as amended) remains a formally fairly restrictive piece of legislation, in regard to access to abortion in practice, the reality has worked out very differently. Despite the fact that the statute deems abortion a criminal offence, that can be legally performed only where two doctors agree it is medically necessary, around one third of women of reproductive age in Britain will at some point have an abortion. Currently, the number of abortions performed to women from England, Wales and Scotland each year stands at around 200,000. Between 1995 and 1998, the number of women terminating pregnancies increased each year (figures for England and Wales were 163,638 in 1995, rising to 177,495 in 1996, to 179,746 in 1997 and 187,402 in 1998). In 1999 the number decreased slightly, and rose again in 2000, to give a total a little below that for 1998. The increase in the abortion rate in the mid-1990s was widely interpreted as a result of the 'Pill panic', but nevertheless, it does seem that women are increasingly prepared to request abortion where the pregnancy is not one they wish to continue.

These figures also suggest that doctors are prepared to interpret the Abortion Act in such a way as to allow women's requests for abortion to be met. For around 200,000 British women who currently legally terminate pregnancy each year, two doctors have authorized that their pregnancy can be ended in line with the terms of the statute. By far the most frequently cited ground for these abortions is that the continuation of the pregnancy constitutes a 'greater threat to the physical or mental health' of the pregnant woman than if it were ended. Most frequently, doctors will judge it the case that the continuation of a pregnancy can constitute a threat to a woman's mental health, if they can identify factors in the woman's life that would stress her if the pregnancy were to continue. In the current context the fact that a pregnancy is, for the woman concerned, unwanted is considered by many doctors a sufficient ground for abortion on this basis. The prestigious Royal College of Obstetricians and Gynaecologists states that abortion is now considered a 'health care need' for women. This interpretation of the terms of the abortion law by doctors is not one that the Government, in the form of the Department of Health, appears opposed to. To the contrary, the 'National Strategy for Sexual Health and HIV Services', published by the Government in 2001 includes comment on the provision of abortion services. This comment makes it clear that it is considered important that limits on women's ability to access abortion services be dealt with as part of a strategy to improve 'sexual health'. For example, variations in the percentage of abortions funded by the NHS in different health authorities and in differences in waiting times for abortion procedures are presented as problematic. The Strategy sets a very ambitious target of all women being able to access an abortion within three weeks of the first appointment with a referring doctor, which, if it is to be achieved, is likely to require a radical overhaul of abortion services, and a significant and costly expansion of them.

Against this background, contributors to *Abortion: Whose Right?* set out their competing answers to this question. While they argue for very different approaches, all agree that even though the issue of abortion is currently deemed 'outside' politics, the developments outlined above are important to discuss and assess. For all contributors, the fact that more women have abortions than in the past tells us something important about the attitudes of women, their partners, doctors and policy makers. What is at issue is how to interpret these attitudes, and whether they constitute indication of movement in a positive or negative direction. Centrally, the reality of demand for abortion and its provision raises questions about the law. Despite politicians' reluctance to consider this issue, the fact that the terms of the statute and the current reality of abortion provision appear to depart significantly, raises issues that merit consideration.

The first three essays reflect on the issue of the law, and the principles that should underpin it. Emily Jackson writes as a legal scholar, concerned with the internal coherence of the law. From this perspective, for Jackson, the 1967 Abortion Act (as amended) is highly problematic. Not only is its coherence undermined by the disparity between the status of abortion as a criminal act and its current provision, it is also clearly contradicted by other developments in medical law. In particular, the emergence of a norm where 'patient autonomy' is deemed central to medical law makes the abortion law anomalous. For Jackson, the situation should be resolved by reforming the statute, to allow autonomy on the part of the pregnant women who chooses abortion to be respected. A polar viewpoint is argued by Helen Watt, who writes in defence of the interests of the unborn. She contends that the moral imperative behind the law must side with defence of the right to life of the unborn, and the autonomy of the pregnant woman does not trump this imperative. For Watt, the fact that the unborn child is located *within* the body of the pregnant woman is of no relevance to its status as a person who should have legal rights. The 'right to life' of the unborn must therefore take priority over the woman's bodily autonomy. The implication of this position is that abortion should be banned by law since it is no different morally to homicide. In the third essay, Theodore Darymple writes as a GP who is critical of the current interpretation of the law by doctors. He outlines his disagreements with advocates of both the 'right to life' of the unborn, and of the importance of autonomy for pregnant women. Given the current context where, for Darymple, it appears the latter viewpoint has in fact triumphed in practice, he discusses mainly his concerns about the concept of 'autonomy'. He strongly criticizes a situation where doctors are simply, for him, conceding to the requests for abortion made by women and, in doing so, are failing to ensure that the moral issues at stake are properly considered by them.

The final two essays focus primarily on what the current demand for abortion tells us about women's lives. Ann Furedi, writing as Director of Communications for the British Pregnancy Advisory Service, Britain's largest specialist provider of abortion, believes that the high demand for abortion should not be considered a problem. In contrast with Darymple, she does not consider it to be the case that the fact that more women than ever have abortions indicates they have not considered the moral issues at stake. Rather, she situates the increasing abortion rate in the context of a society where women expect, and are expected to, make a broader contribution to society than being mothers. An increasing abortion rate in this context, argues Furedi, is unsurprising. She suggests that it is time to remove the stigma from abortion – to think of abortion not as a problem, but as a solution to the problem of unwanted pregnancy for women – and changing the terms in which access to abortion is regulated by law is an important part of doing so. Mary Kenny, in the final essay, offers a different, and less positive interpretation of the current demand for abortion. Writing as a journalist, with a particular interest in the decisions woman make regarding motherhood, she suggests that the ease with which women can now access abortion may not reflect new freedom, so much as new dilemmas for women.

While not arguing that the law should necessarily be more restrictive, neither does Kenny believe its liberalization would be a boon for women. We hope these essays offer readers some new perspectives and ideas on this important social and legal issue.

Essay One

ABORTION: PATIENT AUTONOMY OR MEDICAL PATERNALISM?

Emily Jackson

Abortion occupies a rather curious legal position. It is an exceptionally straightforward and frequently performed operation (in England and Wales approximately 180,000 abortions are carried out each year and about one in three women will have an abortion at some point during their lives), and yet it remains a criminal offence. The Abortion Act 1967 did not abolish the criminal offences of procuring a miscarriage in oneself or another, rather it created a set of tightly circumscribed defences. Neither women having abortions, nor the doctors who perform them will face prosecution provided that the conditions set out in the Abortion Act are satisfied. Outside of the protection offered by these statutory defences, both women and their doctors could face imprisonment. My aim in this essay is to argue that this peculiar legal arrangement is no longer tenable. There are two strands to my argument. First, I suggest that abortion's legalization in 1967 may have been dependent upon abortion retaining its legal status as an inherently morally dubious medical procedure, but that several decades later shifts in attitudes both among the public and within the medical profession mean that this extraordinary legal framework no longer serves any useful purpose. Second, I draw attention to the priority currently afforded to the principle of patient autonomy in other areas of medical practice, and argue that it is time to recognize the pregnant woman's right to decide for herself whether to carry her pregnancy to term.

Currently, as I will explain more fully later, the legality of an abortion is contingent upon professional scrutiny and endorsement of a woman's reasons for wanting to terminate her pregnancy. Underpinning this statutory regime are therefore two assumptions: first, that a woman's reasons for wanting to terminate her pregnancy are a matter of legitimate public interest and, second, that a woman's access to abortion should depend upon whether or not those reasons are deemed acceptable. The crux of my argument will be that both of these assumptions are misguided, and that eligibility for abortion should cease to depend upon whether a woman can persuade two doctors that she has a compelling reason to terminate her unwanted pregnancy.

Questioning the legal relevance of a woman's reasons for seeking an abortion is becoming especially timely and important in the light of the growth in public anxiety that surrounds refinements in prenatal diagnostic techniques. It is already possible to detect fetal sex and a wide range of abnormalities during pregnancy, and the public is fearful that new genetic tests will be devised in order to detect a fetus's predisposition to certain physical characteristics (such as obesity, height and so on) or behavioural traits (such as homosexuality or criminality). Despite general agreement among scientists that this sort of crude genetic determinism is unfounded, there is growing concern that abortion could be used for reasons that many people would consider to be trivial or grounded in prejudice. Insofar as public anxiety about new medical technologies tends to be translated into demands for restrictive regulation, there are likely to be calls for the tightening of the statutory grounds for abortion in order to reflect and reinforce this division between 'deserving' and 'undeserving' reasons for seeking to terminate an unwanted pregnancy.

But while many people instinctively feel that some motives for having an abortion are 'better' than others, I would question whether it is actually possible to distinguish between 'good' and 'bad' reasons with any degree of certainty. Decisions are rarely taken for one single reason, more usually they are informed by a complex and interrelated set of self-regarding and other-regarding motivations. Nor do we make important choices in a social vacuum, rather we commonly take account of the web of relationships within which our lives are embedded. In relation to abortion, a woman will often take into account her relationship with her sexual partner; his feelings about fatherhood; their perception of their capacity to offer a child a supportive and stable home; the impact that a child's birth would have upon her education or career plans and so on. Singling out one of several reasons and then judging it to be either adequate or inadequate wholly misrepresents the collaborative and multifaceted nature of the decision-making process. If it is, in practice, impossible to isolate one reason and subject it to objective evaluation, it makes little sense for eligibility for abortion to be contingent upon precisely this balancing exercise.

THE BACKGROUND TO THE ABORTION ACT 1967

One of the chief strategies adopted by abortion reformers in the 1960s was to draw attention to the implications abortion's illegality had for public health. In 1938, a doctor was acquitted after he had admitted performing an abortion upon a 14-year-old girl who had become pregnant after being gang-raped by a group of soldiers. Because it has always been lawful to carry out an abortion if the pregnant woman would otherwise lose her life, the judge was able to argue that preventing a woman from becoming a 'mental wreck' was tantamount to saving her life, and that it could therefore be lawful to perform a termination where pregnancy was causing a woman intolerable distress. As a result of this decision, before 1967 some doctors were prepared to carry out these 'legal' abortions privately. Safe abortion services did, then, exist prior to the Abortion Act 1967, but they were generally available only to wealthy women and illegal abortions continued to be both common and dangerous. High maternal mortality rates among the poor were therefore a key factor behind abortion's legalization in 1967. Abortion had become a public health issue and there was broad support for bringing it within the safety of medical control. The birth of thousands of children with disabilities caused by thalidomide in the early 1960s may also have furthered the emergence of a climate of public opinion sympathetic to abortion in cases of serious fetal abnormality.

Advocates of legalization argued that when poor women who had already had several children discovered that they were pregnant yet again, they were faced with an invidious choice between having a child who would stretch the family's resources to breaking point, and having an illegal and unsafe abortion, which might deprive their existing children of their primary carer. Reading the parliamentary debates leading up to the passage of the 1967 Act, one finds endless descriptions of the desperate plight of MPs' pregnant constituents who found themselves quite literally 'at the end of their tether'. If both unwanted childbearing *and* backstreet abortions were jeopardizing women's capacity to offer their husbands and children a supportive home life, legal abortion could be said to be necessary in order to protect the health and the sanity of mothers, and thereby to safeguard the well-being and stability of the family.

Given this backdrop, the precise form legalization took is unsurprising. The Abortion Act provides that an abortion is legal if two medical practitioners have formed the opinion, in good faith, that:

- the continuation of the pregnancy poses a risk, greater than if the pregnancy were terminated, to the physical or mental health of the pregnant woman or any existing children of her family; or
- that there is a grave risk to the life or health of the pregnant woman; or
- that, if born, there is a substantial risk that the child would be seriously handicapped.

Unlike the abortion laws of many other countries, these grounds for abortion are rather vague. They do not, for example, specify that an abortion will be legal where the pregnancy has resulted from an act of rape or incest. This ambiguity was undoubtedly deliberate. David Steel's original Abortion Bill had contained clauses specifically allowing abortion where the pregnant woman was under 16 or was pregnant as a result of rape, but these were opposed by both the British Medical Association (BMA) and the Royal College of Obstetricians and Gynaecologists (RCOG). Their fear was that a definitive list of situations in which abortion would be lawful might erode medical discretion, and give women the impression that in certain circumstances abortion would be an *entitlement*.

The legality of an abortion thus lies wholly within the doctors' clinical discretion. Notice that the statute does not even specify that this risk to health must actually *exist*, rather the legality of an abortion is conditional upon whether the doctor has formed the *opinion* that a woman's case fits within the statutory grounds. An abortion would therefore be legal, even if the woman's circumstances did not satisfy the statutory grounds, provided that the two doctors who authorized her termination had acted in good faith. Analogously, a woman whose circumstances plainly satisfy the statutory grounds has no *right* to an abortion; she too is dependent upon first convincing two doctors of the gravity of her plight.

In addition, doctors' participation in the provision of non-emergency abortion services remains entirely voluntary. The Abortion Act 1967 provides medical professionals with a right of conscientious objection to participation in the provision of abortion services, unless the abortion is necessary to save the woman's life.

CRITICISM OF THE ABORTION ACT 1967

While delegating control of abortion to the medical profession may have been a politically astute strategy in 1967, there are reasons to be sceptical about its continued usefulness. Aside from the handful of cases in which an abortion is immediately necessary to save the pregnant woman's life, deciding whether or not to carry an unwanted pregnancy to term is not in fact a medical decision. Doctors may have special expertise in deciding what method should be used, and in carrying out surgical terminations, but they are not necessarily well equipped to predict the impact that having a baby would have upon a particular woman's life. This is, in contrast, a question that the pregnant woman is uniquely well positioned to judge for herself.

Moreover, the logical corollary of giving doctors the power to decide *whether* a pregnancy should be terminated is that there will be times when doctors judge that a woman's situation does not satisfy the statutory grounds, and that an abortion would therefore be unlawful. In such circumstances, the woman is effectively compelled to carry an unwanted pregnancy to term; to go through childbirth against her wishes and, unless the baby is adopted immediately, to assume the onerous responsibilities of parenthood. That this 'involuntary motherhood' is not generally regarded as a violation of the principles – usually dominant in medical law – of bodily autonomy and patient self-determination reveals, I would suggest, a set of dominant assumptions about women's innate and boundless capacity for maternal self-sacrifice.

Of course, it might be argued that pregnant women are not entitled to treat doctors as mere technicians who will perform surgery upon request. Patients never have the *right* to demand that a particular medical procedure is carried out, and this is as true of abortion as it is of any other type of treatment. Yet aside from his conscientious objection, it is not clear upon what grounds a doctor could legitimately refuse to perform a termination. Let me flesh out this claim by considering various possible reasons for refusal.

First, within the NHS there can clearly be no right to expensive medical treatment because scarce resources have made rationing decisions inevitable. Health authorities make largely discretionary funding decisions, and these have proved remarkably resilient to legal challenge. However, an abortion will always cost the NHS much less than a woman's pregnancy and delivery, so a doctor's refusal to co-operate with a woman's request for abortion could not be justified on grounds of cost. Even if we completely disregard any expenses incurred after the child's birth, carrying the average pregnancy to term will cost a health authority approximately seven times as much as the average abortion.

Alternatively, a doctor might argue that abortion is not in a woman's *clinical* interest. But it is actually extremely difficult to imagine any circumstances in which a doctor's *clinical* judgement could lead him to deny a woman's request for abortion. Even abortions carried out in the third trimester of pregnancy will usually be less risky than childbirth. So if carrying a pregnancy to term invariably poses a greater risk to the health of a woman than an abortion, it is not clear how a refusal to carry out a termination could advance the woman's *physical* health. If the woman has decided that she does not want to be pregnant, her mental well-being is also unlikely to be furthered by compelling her to carry her unwanted pregnancy to term. Despite the claims made by the anti-abortion movement, in practice few women experience regret or distress after having an abortion. The more common reaction is relief. And in any event, the possibility that someone might have a change of heart is not – in itself – a sufficient reason for preventing them from making the decision in the first place. Otherwise we should not allow people to decide for themselves whether to get married or be sterilized, since both are choices that may subsequently be regretted.

In short, it is difficult to imagine how a doctor could deny a woman access to abortion on either clinical or financial grounds. Added to this, since doctors have the right to refuse to participate in services on purely moral grounds, and therefore do not need to invoke the statutory defences in order to give effect to their personal consciences, what other basis could there be for a doctor's decision that a woman's circumstances do not justify abortion?

Could it be said, for example, that the medical profession is charged with protecting fetal life, which the law recognizes as worthy of some legal protection, while falling short of full personhood? Here it becomes helpful to contrast abortion with certain other medical procedures carried out during pregnancy, in which the principle of patient self-determination has prevailed over concern for fetal life. Central to medical law is the principle of patient autonomy, according to which every competent adult patient has an absolute right to decide whether or not to accept medical treatment. Within the last few years a series of cases involving women who have refused to consent to Caesarean delivery has confirmed that this right is not diminished where the woman's decision might lead not only to her own death, but also to that of her fetus. As one judge explained:

> ... a competent woman, who has the capacity to decide, may, for religious reasons, other reasons, for rational or irrational reasons or for no reason at all, choose not to have medical intervention, even though the consequence may be the death or serious handicap of the child she bears or her own death.

So it is clear that in the context of a *refusal* of medical treatment, the life of a full-term fetus is judged less important than safeguarding the woman's right to make decisions about her body, even where her reasons for taking a particular decision are foolish, immoral or non-existent.

There is, of course, a difference between respecting a woman's refusal of surgical intervention, and deliberately killing a fetus. In essence, this is the act/omission distinction, according to which intentionally acting to end life is judged more culpable than failing to save it. Thus, a doctor who performs an abortion deliberately *acts* positively to end fetal life, whereas a doctor who respects his pregnant patient's refusal to consent to a Caesarean section does not intend the fetus's death, nor does he directly cause it. However, despite its apparent clarity and moral simplicity, the act/omission distinction does not offer a compelling justification for medical control over abortion. In relation to decisions about euthanasia and the withdrawal of medical treatment, for example, differentiating between acts and omissions has led to some rather dubious and arbitrary distinctions. (A doctor who withdraws an artificial feeding tube has *omitted* to act, whereas a malicious interloper doing exactly the same thing would be judged to have *acted* positively to end the patient's life.) Moreover, as the Abortion Act makes clear, it can of course be perfectly lawful to deliberately act to end fetal life, so the first principles of medical ethics that result in a clear and absolute rule against deliberately acting to end a *person*'s life already do not apply to fetuses. Given abortion's legality, the act/omission distinction cannot explain why doctors need to be charged with policing a woman's reasons for wanting to terminate her pregnancy.

The protection offered to fetal life by the Abortion Act is, in short, that doctors have a right to veto a woman's decision to terminate her pregnancy if they do not believe that she has an adequate reason for doing so. But surely this would be a moral rather than a clinical decision, and one that is adequately protected by giving doctors the right to exclude themselves from the provision of abortion services. If a doctor thinks that a woman exhibits a cavalier attitude towards fetal life, he is perfectly entitled to invoke his conscientious objection to abortion and refuse to have anything to do with her treatment.

Making abortion's legality contingent upon what must be a subjective moral judgement may have served a useful strategic purpose for abortion reformers in the 1960s, but the medical profession itself now recognizes it to be wholly inappropriate. Both the BMA and the RCOG have acknowledged that doctors' role in abortion decision-making should no longer consist in judging the legitimacy of a woman's reasons for abortion. The BMA's latest guidance to doctors states that:

> ... [d]octors with a conscientious objection to abortion should make their views known to the patient and enable the patient to see another doctor without delay if that is the patient's wish.

Similarly, in its most recent guideline on induced abortion, the RCOG recommends that a doctor who is reluctant to assist a woman who requests an abortion should simply refer her to a colleague who will be able to help her. The need for pregnancy to pose a greater risk to her well-being than abortion is, the RCOG points out, satisfied in *every* unwanted pregnancy.

It could, of course, be argued that the Abortion Act simply contains a harmless legal fiction because, in practice, doctors usually just give their *approval* for decisions that have already been taken. Why then should we worry about a statute that is commonly interpreted so liberally that it has little impact upon the provision of abortion services? Despite the comparative ease with which most women can gain access to abortion services, for a number of reasons I believe that the requirement that a woman must first satisfy two doctors that she has compelling grounds to terminate her pregnancy should nevertheless be removed from the legislation.

First, it is impossible to tell how many women are given misleading advice about their eligibility for abortion. Doctors are under no duty to publicize their conscientious objection to abortion and so some women undoubtedly mistake their doctor's reluctance to co-operate as an indication of their ineligibility for termination, rather than an expression of their doctor's moral convictions. Additionally, women from ethnic minority groups or women who are poorly educated may not have the knowledge or the confidence to seek a second opinion if their general practitioner seems obstructive, and women from rural areas faced with an unsympathetic doctor may not easily be able to find an alternative medical practitioner. Even if a woman does seek another opinion, her encounter with a hostile doctor will invariably delay her abortion. Of course, if a woman is able to find and afford a private abortion clinic, she will not encounter any doctors with conscientious objections to abortion and will therefore have access to a prompt and supportive service. Inevitably then, the Abortion Act's entrenched deference to medical opinion has disproportionate practical impact upon the choices of poorer women.

Second, a woman who wants an abortion must present her circumstances in the worst possible light in order to persuade two medical practitioners that continuing the pregnancy would threaten her mental or physical well-being. Eligibility for abortion in the UK is therefore contingent upon women describing their circumstances as difficult or desperate. The Abortion Act 1967 requires women who want to terminate their unwanted pregnancies to first wrestle with the supposed trauma of abortion, thus reinforcing the assumption that the desire to terminate an unwanted pregnancy is culturally unacceptable unless accompanied by an acknowledgement of maternal instinct and psychological distress. Underpinning the 1967 Act is the presumption that motherhood is *always* an easier choice for women than abortion, as though maternal self-sacrifice is innate and instinctive. The Act implies that, by putting her own life plan first, the woman seeking an abortion automatically reveals herself to be troubled and perhaps even unbalanced. But we no longer believe that a desire not to be pregnant is evidence of mental instability, and it is clearly undesirable that legislation should rely upon and reinvigorate this sort of damaging gender stereotype.

Third, there are times when a woman may need medical advice in order to decide whether or not to terminate her pregnancy. As the number of predictive genetic tests increases, so does the proportion of pregnant women who may be given complex prenatal diagnoses. Genetic tests that give a simple yes/no answer are the exception. Results may instead offer a prediction of susceptibility to *future* ill-health. In order to digest and evaluate probabilistic genetic test results, pregnant women may need professional help, and in practice expert medical advice is commonly sought in order to translate ambiguous information into intelligible advice. In such circumstances, I would suggest that a medical professional's twin roles as impartial counsellor *and* as the ultimate authority over abortion decision-making could undermine the doctor–patient relationship.

While information derived from prenatal tests may assist informed decision-making by pregnant women, where that information is predictive of future risk, a productive dialogue between doctors and their patients might be of particular importance. Collaborative decision-making is not, however, fostered by the remarkable authority vested in doctors by the Abortion Act 1967. As we have seen, the statute gives doctors a right to veto women's abortion decisions. So if a woman decides during specialist genetic counselling sessions that she does not want to carry her pregnancy to term, that decision cannot stand unless it is subsequently approved by two doctors. Where a pregnant woman has been advised by her obstetrician, he/she may be responsible both for helping a woman to come to a decision *and then judging its adequacy*. That the facilitator of a decision should also exercise a right of veto over that decision is, perhaps, undesirable. It could therefore plausibly be argued that the extraordinary control doctors exercise over the decision to terminate an unwanted pregnancy might either disrupt their capacity to offer sensitive and productive advice about the results of genetic tests, or undermine the finality of specialist genetic counselling.

CONCLUSION

To sum up, the regulation of abortion in the UK reflects the social and political context in which it was legalized. The Abortion Act's delegation of decision-making authority to the medical profession may have been necessary in order to galvanize parliamentary support for legalisation in 1967. Several decades later, attitudes towards abortion have changed and the law now seems rather outdated. The

RCOG has advised its members that women should be entitled to prompt access to abortion services, and that abortion should now be treated as a routine and non-controversial aspect of medical care. Yet, as we have seen, abortion remains a criminal offence. A woman has no right to terminate an unwanted pregnancy, and must instead depend entirely upon the beneficent exercise of medical discretion. While this might be comparatively unimportant if the statute was working satisfactorily, the practical impact of abortion's continued medicalization is to restrict the reproductive choices of disadvantaged women.

Moreover, we should consider whether the law's extraordinary treatment of abortion sits uneasily with the rest of British medical law. In particular, the Act's insistence upon two doctors deciding whether a woman should be able to terminate an unwanted pregnancy may be out of step with the increasing priority given to a patient's right to make their own decisions about their medical treatment. According to the Abortion Act, if two doctors do *not* consider that the statutory grounds are satisfied, an abortion would be unlawful, and the woman is compelled to carry her unwanted pregnancy to term. But pregnancy, especially in its later stages, is an exceptionally invasive and often painful experience, and giving birth automatically leads to the onerous and enduring responsibilities of motherhood. Insofar as a non-consensual operation is illegitimate because it would interfere with a person's right to make important decisions about their life according to their own values, relationships and priorities, requiring a pregnant woman to become a mother against her wishes might be similarly disruptive.

In the light of the increasing availability of prenatal tests, it is particularly important that the doctor–patient relationship is not skewed by the Abortion Act's uneven distribution of decision-making authority. Increasingly women may need help in order to digest complex information about genetic risk. This sort of assistance is not necessarily best provided within a legislative framework that endows doctors with the right to veto women's abortion decisions. So, in addition to improving abortion law's congruence with the principle of patient autonomy, giving women greater freedom to make their own decisions about termination might be an important adjunct of a shift towards a model of medical decision-making based upon partnership rather than power.

Essay Two

LIVING TOGETHER: PREGNANCY AND PARENTHOOD
Helen Watt

In this essay, I will look at arguments for and against abortion: arguments concerning the right to control one's own body, the right to immunity from bodily attacks, and stages in development such as viability or the capacity for rational thought which have been suggested as the point when human life acquires serious moral status.

Before focusing on these moral arguments, it is worth noting that abortion raises emotional, as well as intellectual problems. Many people are personally affected by abortion, or fear they may need to resort to abortion at some time in the future (for example, if their contraception fails). The idea that abortion could be morally wrong is one which may be personally very challenging. What would it mean? That we would need to look again at our own past abortions? At our sexual relationships? Accept any child we may conceive in the future, however difficult that may be? Change our job, if there is a link to abortion? Alienate our friends?

It is tempting at this point to bypass the moral question altogether, by saying that abortion is 'necessary' for women – a 'fact of life'. After all, women have projects and commitments which are not always compatible with pregnancy and childbirth at any given time. They need to be able to plan their lives, as men do, without fear of having their plans overturned by biological events. And without easy access to abortion, will we not have unplanned and unwanted children – and, indeed, women killed or injured by backstreet abortions?

These are serious questions, which I will return to later on. Here it is enough to say that the moral question of abortion cannot be bypassed simply by saying that abortion is necessary. If it really is the case that the fetus is a child, as opponents of abortion claim, it will be very hard to say that it is necessary to take that child's life. We might think here of street children in Brazil, who are literally shot by those who want to 'clear the streets' of their unwanted presence. To kill such children on the grounds that they are unwanted by parents or society is clearly not acceptable: we need to respond in a very different way to the social challenge they pose. Similarly, if the fetus is a child – a possibility which has to be confronted – we will need to find non-violent ways of responding to its presence, however unwelcome that presence may at first be.

 CONTROLLING OUR BODIES

There is another way of preempting the question of the status of the fetus, which is to say that a woman has an absolute right to control her own body. The fetus is located within, and dependent on, the body of the pregnant woman. Even assuming that the fetus is a 'person' or human being, with all the rights that this involves, surely no other person has the right to make use of another person's body?

This may seem initially plausible: your body may seem like 'property' over which you have total control. When we look more closely, however, we see that *any* form of support for another person will involve your body in some way. This applies whether you are breastfeeding a baby, spoon-feeding a disabled brother or sister, or even writing a cheque for the hostel down the road. So does that mean you need not support anyone – not even members of your own family – just because your body is involved? You may not have *chosen* to have a brother or sister, or a newborn child who needs you, but not all moral obligations are chosen: many simply arise. If you were to let your baby starve to death, because you were unwilling to feed it and no one else could take your place, it would be a poor excuse to say that you never *chose* to have a child depending on your body. So why is it any more acceptable to withdraw bodily support before the child is born?

◇ ● ●
● ●
● ● ◇ **BODILY ATTACKS**

Moreover, abortion is not, in many cases, a mere withdrawal of bodily support. To begin with, the aim of abortion, whatever the method used, will often be to destroy the fetus, not simply to remove it from the woman's body. Often the woman and the doctor performing the abortion do not simply want to stop the woman being pregnant; they want there not to be a baby in the world for whom they are responsible. Thus, in the case of a late abortion performed by inducing labour, the fetus is often injected beforehand with the poison potassium chloride, precisely to ensure that it does not survive being born.

Even if the aim is not to kill the unborn child, abortion will still very often involve a deliberate attack on the child's body. For example, in abortion by vacuum aspiration, a very common form of early abortion, the baby is sucked piecemeal down the tube. At the end of the procedure, the nurse has the unpleasant task of reconstructing the body to make sure no parts are left inside the woman's womb. The woman herself may not be aware of just what her abortion will involve: euphemisms such as 'the contents of the uterus' are often used. However, it is clear that this procedure is not a mere 'removal' of the fetus from the womb.

We need to ask: does not the fetus – assuming it has the moral status of a human being – have a right to have its body respected, and not deliberately attacked? Undeniably, it does have this right, if it has full human status. Just as the woman has a right not to have her body attacked – for example, poisoned or pulled apart – the same is true of her unborn child.

◈ ● ●
● ●
● ● ◈ **CONDEMNING WOMEN?**

There is no avoiding the central moral question posed by abortion: does the fetus have the moral status of any human being? Before looking at this question, however, there is one point which needs to be made clear. It is often assumed that any suggestion that abortion is morally unjustified implies a harsh and hostile view of those who have abortions. This is not the case: there are many reasons why a woman who has an abortion may not be fully aware of what abortion involves. And even if she were aware, this does not mean she should be harshly judged by other people. Abortion is arguably at least as harmful for the woman herself as it is for her child: women who have had abortions need more, not less, support on that account. (Such support is available in Britain from organizations such as British Victims of Abortion, which are run by women who have had abortions themselves.)

STATUS OF THE FETUS

I will return later to the impact that abortion has on women. In the meantime, how should we deal with the question of the status of the fetus? A frequent suggestion is that 'viability', or the capacity to survive outside the womb, is what gives a child status. However, this is simply to assert that the weak (or the weakest) have no moral claim on the strong – which is not what we say about born human beings who are weak and dependent. To say that a newborn child is 'less human' than we are, just because it needs the help of others, would be morally outrageous. Strength and size can never determine the status of any human being. And we all owe our lives to the fact that we were cared for and respected when we were small and weak and dependent ourselves.

We should remember that viability depends on the medical facilities available for premature babies: a baby who is viable in a modern Western hospital may not be viable in an African village. Can a child's moral status depend on the mere fact of where it is located? And why should a child have a serious moral claim on the pregnant woman only at the point when it is strong enough to live outside her body? Similar questions arise in relation to the claim that the fetus does not have human status because so many unborn children naturally miscarry. Do we say that terminal patients have a lower moral status than other human beings, just because they may die naturally within a few weeks? What has strength to do with status?

Again, some people claim that the fetus is not a human being until it is *visibly and obviously* human. However, no one would deny that a child with serious facial deformities was as much a human being as a child of more conventional appearance. 'Human' appearance makes no difference to a child's moral status, any more than size or strength. (In any case, the fetus *does* 'look human' from surprisingly early on in pregnancy. Even a very young embryo 'looks human' to those who know what a human individual looks like at that stage in its life.) There are, of course, differences in structure and appearance between embryo and fetus, fetus and infant, infant and toddler, and so on. But why should these differences have any relevance to that individual's moral status?

Some see the fetus as having human status only when the mother has bonded with the fetus: has come to see it as her child. A wanted fetus is a 'person', on this view, while an unwanted fetus is not. The problem here is that we do not normally think that people are only morally significant when other people come to see them as such. What would we say about those who refuse to recognize people of other races, or those with disabilities: are such people not human, in the moral sense, until they are *recognized* as human? Humanity makes demands on us which are objective: it is not up to us to confer human status or withdraw it when we choose.

LIVING HUMAN PERSONS

Some say that only those human beings or 'persons' who are currently capable of, for example, rational thought have full moral status. This would also exclude newborn babies from the moral category of 'person' – but some claim that babies, too, are morally 'subpersonal', and have no right to life. After all, babies cannot think rationally, or set a value on their own lives, any more than unborn children.

This approach fails, however, to recognize the *bodily nature* of the human moral subject. We are not purely spiritual beings, even if we have a spiritual aspect. Rather, we are living human organisms:

animals of a special kind. We belong to the rational human species, and are fulfilled by (among other things) using the powers we have to develop rational abilities. To ask when the human being or person begins, we should ask when the human animal begins. The answer to this will normally be: at fertilization. Admittedly, not every embryo is created at fertilization: twins can be created when cells are separated from an existing embryo. However, whether an embryo is created from sperm and egg, or from cells of an existing embryo, each embryo is the first stage in the life-cycle of a human being.

Once we accept that the embryo is a human individual at the start of its life, the way is open to recognize the interests of the embryo (and fetus and infant) in its own future well-being. *Having* an interest in one's own well-being is different from *taking* an interest. Imagine a 16-year-old girl with brain damage that will heal itself within nine months. The girl is deeply unconscious and cannot take an interest in her own health. Nor can she take an interest in other things which require her to be healthy, or at least, rational and conscious – for example, in going to university, making new friends, and so on. However, she *has* an interest in her own health (for example, if there is some possible treatment, she will have an interest in that treatment). She also has an interest in the things health makes possible – study, friendships and so on – in that these things are good for the kind of being she is. Even if her body cannot heal itself, and even if it cannot be healed by medical treatment, she will still have an interest in health and other things which are good for human beings. The same is true of an unborn child, who does not normally need to heal from damage, but merely needs to grow up in a family to have rational abilities.

We need to remember that *people* are morally important, not just their thoughts and feelings. In fact, thoughts and feelings are important precisely because they are good (or potentially good) for the human being who has them. It is good for me, as an embryo, fetus, and infant, to grow up to have thoughts and feelings of a kind I cannot have for many years. If the fetus is me, why is it not bad for me to be deprived of my life? And why is it not morally wrong for me to be *deliberately* deprived of my life – at least if I am innocent of crime or aggression?

ABORTION AND DISABILITY

Some say that if the fetus is going to be disabled, and especially if it will suffer, its life may not be worth living, so that abortion in this case may be justified. However, to say this is to devalue the lives of disabled people who are already born – as many disabled people have themselves pointed out. Are we going to kill born disabled people too, because we think their lives are not worthwhile? Should we not value the presence of all human beings, whatever their state of health? Of course we can always 'prevent disability' by killing those who are disabled. However, this is no more acceptable in Britain today than it was in Germany in the 1930s, when the disabled were indeed killed as a 'burden' to themselves and the State. It is not right to treat human beings as subhuman, or their lives as having no value, whether on the ground of disability, age, size or level of development. There is no such thing as a 'worthless' human life.

Some claim that disability is (or can be) so burdensome for the family of the disabled person that this alone justifies abortion of a disabled unborn child. This approach tends to underestimate the suffering involved in losing a child by late abortion – to say nothing of the risk of miscarriage caused by tests used to detect medical conditions in the womb. It also fails to recognize what countless families of disabled children have discovered for themselves: that the disabled child can be experienced as a blessing – a gift which enriches the family. There is much we can learn from the experience of caring for a disabled child about the meaning of life, and of love as unconditional acceptance. In contrast, what we learn from abortion is that children need not be accepted unconditionally – and may even be killed if they fail to meet our standards of health.

ABORTION AND MEDICINE

Abortion is not, as some practitioners would claim, a straightforward medical procedure. Rather, it is the very reverse of medicine, which heals and supports human beings. This has implications for the doctor who faces a request for an abortion. Should doctors carry out their patients' orders blindly, no matter how harmful this will be to the patient or to others? We are rightly horrified by the practice of female circumcision in some Muslim countries. However, we unthinkingly accept the violence done to healthy women and their unborn children in our own hospitals and clinics. Pregnancy is not a disease, and abortion is not a cure. It does not heal a woman, but rather harms her, preventing her completing a vital human task: a task no less important for the fact that it is so often undervalued. To see the fetus as an 'invading organism' (as one abortion advocate describes it) is to take a deeply distorted view of the natural and intimate bond between a pregnant woman and her child. The child is not seen as a son or daughter, who needs the protection of its mother. It is seen as the enemy: an alien and hostile force, which needs to be violently subdued.

WOMEN'S INTERESTS

Abortion is not in a woman's interests, either medically or psychologically. Society should change to fit women's (and men's) fertility, by supporting men and women in their responsibilities as parents. Instead, we change the bodies of women to make them non-pregnant, and therefore in need of less support. But having children is a valuable social contribution, not a private project of women to be carried out at their own risk. There is a tendency for men, for example, to wash their hands of women who decide to go through with their pregnancies – for is that not their choice? The child's father may wonder why he is expected to contribute child support: after all, he did not, unlike the woman, 'choose' to have a child. Men, more than women, are encouraged by abortion to think of themselves as having 'commitment-free' sex: a sexual relationship with no parental dimension, and with no strings attached.

It comes as a surprise to many people to learn that feminists in the nineteenth century were strongly opposed to abortion, which they saw as harmful to the woman, as well as to her child. Now, in the twenty-first century, we have ample evidence of the harm abortion does to women, in the stories of so many women who regret their abortions. Abortion is not a strong and protective choice, but a choice of weakness and fear. It is a rejection by women of their own creative and protective powers: a failure to meet the challenge of parenthood, a failure to defend one's own child. Many women have abortions in situations where they themselves see abortion as morally wrong, and struggle for years with feelings of anger, depression and guilt as a result. Those who regret their abortions will often report that it took years for them to come to terms with their feelings: only after years of 'blocking off' their emotions could they admit to themselves and to others what their abortion really meant. To treat abortion as a solution to the problems women face is to fail to recognize its impact not only on the child but on the woman herself.

◈ ● ●
● ●
● ● ◈ **LEGAL ISSUES**

How, then, should the legal system respond to the practice of abortion? If it is true that abortion is lethal to one human being, and also harmful to another, this is not something towards which the law can afford to be indifferent. We all expect the law to protect us from homicide at the age we are now. We also expect the law to protect those who are younger and more vulnerable than ourselves – for example, newborn babies. So why should the law not protect those who are still younger and still more vulnerable – to say nothing of protecting their mothers from a harmful, non-therapeutic procedure?

We are not talking here of truly medical procedures, where the baby dies as a side-effect of treatment for its mother. An example might be a hysterectomy on a pregnant, but cancerous womb, where the baby's death is foreseen, but not intended, in operating on the pregnant woman. Another example would be the removal of a fallopian tube which has been damaged by an ectopic pregnancy: in this case, the tube would need to be removed even if the child had already miscarried. The aim here is not to attack the life or body of the child, but merely to remove a damaged organ of the mother which is threatening her life. Clearly, to foresee that a child will die as a side-effect of treating its mother is something very different from deliberately aiming at that child's death.

BACKSTREET ABORTION

It is often said that making abortion illegal will result in many women dying every year from backstreet abortions. In fact, if we look at figures for maternal deaths, in Britain and elsewhere, we see that they were falling in number before permissive laws on abortion were passed, and went on falling at a similar rate after the passing of such laws. It was better medical care, such as the use of antibiotics, that reduced maternal deaths. Of course, there will always be some illegal abortions, whatever the law on abortion. However, the same can be said of other forms of violence, such as child abuse or rape. Would we make these practices legal, just because they still go on, despite laws against them?

UNWANTED CHILDREN

The argument that we must avoid the birth of unwanted children, who will then be ill-treated by their parents, is also not supported by the facts. Leaving aside the logic of killing a child to protect it from abuse, child abuse rates have gone up, not down, with the legalization of abortion. In contrast, it is well-known that parents who were horrified to learn of a pregnancy can be delighted once the child has been born. While adoption is, of course, a possibility for those who really cannot cope with a child, most people are able to cope with, and love, their own children. If they can be helped through the initial period of rejection, whether by friends or family or by counsellors, they can be very affectionate parents, even if they still need support.

 **CONCLUSION**

What has happened to society, more than three decades after the passing of the Abortion Act in Britain? Society has not become more welcoming of children, or more celebratory of pregnancy. Women have not been encouraged to accept, and use responsibly, their reproductive powers, but have rather been encouraged to reject both their children and themselves as parents. In the same way, men have been encouraged to back away from their responsibilities for their partners and their children.

Medicine has not become more respectful of human life; instead, abortion has been joined by embryo experimentation, and by an increasing willingness to terminate lives of 'low quality'. Instead of serving the health of their patients, and supporting those who cannot be cured, doctors increasingly see themselves as mere technicians serving patients' desires.

With the advent of legal abortion, thousands of children have lost their lives at the hands of such doctors: children who would have loved us, and whom we would have loved. Every abortion is a human tragedy for the child and for its mother: a tragedy which could, and should, have been avoided. No child can be replaced by a child born later. Every child is an individual, with its own future to respect.

In the area of abortion, the hard questions must be faced, without seeking refuge in slogans or in knee-jerk reactions. Abortion is a major social injustice, directed at those who are most vulnerable. Many people have a vested interest – whether personal or financial – in this injustice not being challenged. We must look behind the euphemisms used to describe abortion, which themselves testify to people's bad conscience on abortion, to what it really means for the woman, and what it means for her child. Children are not possessions under our control, at any stage of their existence. We should learn to live in peace with our children, for the nine months when they first need us – remembering that we ourselves enjoyed the peace and safety of the womb at the start of our lives.

Essay Three

THE DEMORALIZATION OF ABORTION
Theodore Darymple

The permissibility or otherwise of abortion – the deliberate termination of a pregnancy – is generally discussed as a matter of competing rights. Does the right of the mother to control the course of her life trump that of the fetus (or embryo) to life itself? Once this question has been answered, at least to the satisfaction of the person asking it, no further problem is thought to arise: an indubitably correct answer has been found.

The outlines of the dispute are clear. Those who view the fertilized ovum as a full member of the human community, entitled morally to the same protection as any other human being, consider abortion to be murder pure and simple, as reprehensible as, say, the stabbing to death of a woman in a post office queue. Those who, on the other hand, hold that the embryo is not a human being because it has neither consciousness nor self-consciousness, consider the destruction of its life as being no more problematic morally than, say, the expulsion of a parasitic tapeworm. Hence if a woman wants to end a pregnancy – for whatever reason – she has a perfect right to do so. As sovereign of her own body, she has the determining, indeed the only, say as to what should be done to it.

As we shall see, the competition between absolute rights is a crude way in which to approach this, or indeed any, moral question. For the moment, however, let us examine the difficulties of both positions outlined above.

THE PROBLEM WITH RIGHTS

It is surely not plausible to assert that the embryo or fetus is as worthy of the same moral and emotional regard as a more developed human being. One would not expect parents to mourn a natural miscarriage in the same way that they might mourn the death of a five-year-old child: indeed, were they to do so, we should consider them mildly deranged or even morally depraved. And any principle, such as that the destruction of an embryo is equal to the murder of a child or an adult, that does considerable violence to our natural feelings, is not likely to be useful as a guide to how we should behave. Enshrined into law, it will almost inevitably result in widespread evasion and disobedience.

Of course, the person who holds that the embryo should be as protected by law as the fully formed human manages thereby to avoid the argument from the slippery slope. But moral consistency brings with it equal problems. If all forms of human life, from the embryo to the centenarian, are utterly sacrosanct, then killing in any circumstances is wrong. But few people, apart from a small band of resist-not-evil Tolstoyans, actually hold this view. If a man hijacks an aircraft and threatens to fly it into a large building full of people, but could be prevented if he were himself killed, few would regard his death as being other than desirable, or even morally obligatory for those in a position to bring it about. In other words, while it is obviously desirable that we should in general hold human life to be sacrosanct, there are circumstances in which we need not, or even should not, do so. The argument is about the circumstances, not the principle.

The denial of full human status to the embryo or fetus because it has no self-consciousness and therefore no interests that need protection, also runs into difficulty if the principle upon which the denial is based is applied consistently. There are plenty of other human beings who are not self-conscious and therefore have no interests that require protection: those who are asleep, for example, or those who are temporarily unconscious through an accident. Is the murder of a sleeping man any the less a murder because he is asleep? It is true that the victim is potentially self-conscious and therefore potentially has interests: but the same is true of the embryo, in whose case the argument from potentiality has been rejected.

Moreover, in arguing that it is personhood, not human life itself, to which rights attach, defenders of abortion raise further difficulties. It is clear that the self-conscious person whose life is, in their opinion, endowed with rights (unlike that of the embryo) grows slowly and gradually into personhood. There is no clear dividing line or instant in a human life, before which the human being was not a person and after which he or she is a person. But even defenders of abortion agree that the killing has to stop at some point (though there are those who have gone as far as approving of infanticide up to six months): and since any cut-off point on a continuum is to an extent arbitrary, it is as difficult for pro as for anti-abortionists to be entirely consistent with their basic theoretical principle.

However, supporters of abortion (at least, of abortion on demand) rely not just on the lack of moral status of the human embryo or fetus, but upon the supposed right of the woman to personal autonomy. This autonomy includes the right to decide whether or not to continue with a pregnancy once it has started. She has the right to choose, because it is her life that is so profoundly affected.

THE FICTION OF AUTONOMY

There are several observations that need to be made. The right in question is regarded by its advocates as absolute, unconditional and inalienable, regardless of such considerations as ability to pay, or indeed of any other considerations. But if a woman has such an absolute 'right' to an abortion – that is to say, the right to a termination of pregnancy in modern and safe medical conditions – someone is under an obligation to provide it. Does this mean it would be perfectly reasonable for the state, in certain cases, to coerce doctors into performing abortions, regardless of their personal convictions or opinions about the individual cases? Surely this could not be a right that the state has.

The right to autonomy is widely touted these days as being a philosopher's stone of medical ethics, but it is largely a right of veto rather than a right to whatever treatment the patient wishes to have. The patient can, of course, choose whether or not to go to the doctor when he is ill; he can likewise choose to accept or not any of the treatments that he is offered by the doctor (except in certain circumstances, where he has an infectious disease that, left untreated, would constitute a public health hazard, or where the balance of his mind is disturbed and he is no longer capable of making a reasonable choice). But the right to autonomy does not – or should not – include the right to demand of the doctor any drug or surgical treatment that the patient would like.

Let us suppose that a patient, believing himself to possess an absolute right to personal autonomy, went to a doctor and demanded that the doctor cut off a perfectly healthy arm or ear. The doctor would naturally ask why he wanted such an operation. The patient would not feel obliged to provide an explanation: his answer that 'It's my right' would seem to him quite sufficient. And if he really did possess such a right, it would indeed constitute a perfect answer. The fact that he wanted – or demanded – the operation would be enough. In a regime of complete personal autonomy, whim is law.

The role of the doctor in any civilized country, however, is not just that of executor of his patient's wishes, irrespective of what they might be. The doctor advises and guides: he is not just a provider of medical wares, amongst which his patient chooses indiscriminately. The appeal to the concept of autonomy, therefore, is not sufficient to establish a 'right' to abortion. A doctor should not be able to force an abortion on a woman; but this does not mean that a woman should be able to force an abortion on a doctor. One person's autonomy is another's compulsion.

What, in any case, do people mean when they say they have a right to something? Increasingly, they do not mean permission to do or to have something that is temporarily granted to them by the supreme political power in the jurisdiction in which they happen to live: a permission that can just as well be removed as granted. Instead, they mean something altogether more metaphysical, free-floating above all other considerations whatsoever, an inalienable permission that it is quite beyond the moral power of anyone or any legislature to withhold or abrogate: something that arrives *pari passu* with the capacity to breathe.

But where do these rights come from? They can hardly be called self-evident, because the pretended right to abortion, for example, has been denied by the great majority of people throughout human history who have given the matter thought. For a proposition to be called self-evident, it must be evident to other than the person claiming it to be so.

Rights could, of course, be conferred by a supreme being, that is to say by God. The problem with this view is that it not only depends upon a belief in the existence of such a supreme being, which is far from universally shared nowadays, least of all by those with a belief in the right to abortion, but it depends upon a certain specific interpretation of God's will. I am no theologian, but I doubt if there is any scripture in the world that unequivocally grants the right to abortion to any woman who wants one. Insofar as God has spoken through the mouths of men, it is to condemn the practice *in toto*.

How is a right, in the metaphysically absolute sense in which the word is now used, to be discovered? That rights have to be discovered is clear, because the right to abortion had not been heard of in 1960, any more than America had been heard of in 1473. At best, like the western continent, it was a vague rumour that circulated among theorists who were regarded as being not altogether in their right minds. Do we send out daring explorers into hitherto unexplored metaphysical realms, who bring us back treasures that were there all along, like the silver and gold of the Indies? Who is this Columbus of human rights?

RIGHTS AND MORALITY

There was a time, no doubt, when the concept of rights helped to curb and restrain the exercise of arbitrary power. But the rights that do this – the right to a fair trial, for example, or the right to free speech – are derived from values that we hold, and are certainly not the free-standing source of those values.

The right to a fair trial is valuable because we desire justice: we do not desire justice because every man has a right to a fair trial. And if anyone were to deny the right to a fair trial, we should not know how to answer him, because he would in effect be arguing that arbitrary or capricious exculpation and punishment were acceptable or even desirable.

The right to freedom of speech arises from our desire for freedom in general, and from the belief that, whatever the inconveniences that sometimes attend it, free speech both gives meaning to life and is of practical value, since truth is more likely to emerge from a clash of opinion than from a uniformly imposed set of beliefs. As with the right to a fair trial, the right to free speech is secondary to a value already held: it is not the origin of that value.

Moreover, freedom of speech is not absolute. It is circumscribed by the laws of libel. For example, sedition and incitement are likewise not permitted. Even the right to a fair trial may be abrogated in certain circumstances. This is because there is no one value that is superordinate to all other values, and values may – indeed, often do – clash. We often sacrifice one value to another, as the situation demands. We value free speech, but in times of war it may be necessary to curb enemy propaganda. We value both freedom and safety, but we cannot be both completely free and completely safe. The mountaineer cannot both climb his mountains and be assured of never suffering a broken leg.

The problem with the doctrine of rights, at least in its modern form, is not only theoretical (the question of their origin being unanswered, indeed unasked), but practical. For the effect of the doctrine is to coarsen not only moral discourse, but moral sensibilities and even behaviour. For a right to be truly a right in the metaphysical sense – the sense in which people who say 'I know my rights' almost always use the word – it must transcend all other considerations. If a man has a right to a roof over his head, then no conduct on his part can deprive him of such a roof. He must be housed, though he has destroyed a thousand houses. So it is with all other rights: and if enough such rights are believed to exist, and moreover are treated as if they really did exist, it is clear that one of the great motives of good conduct, the fear of the consequences of bad conduct, is removed. But hope cannot long survive the downfall of fear: and thus life loses all meaning whatsoever.

If an action falls within the metaphysical right of a man to perform it, then the action requires no further moral justification. The metaphysical conception of rights halts all further or deeper moral enquiry. But real life is not, or should not be, like this. The ability of our legal rights to inform us what we should or should not do is very limited. For example, I have the right to buy a painting by Rembrandt, if I have enough money. Once such a painting is in my possession I have the legal right to destroy or deface it, if I so desire: but surely no one would argue by way of exculpation or even mitigation, were I to do so, that I had acted within my rights. My rights have nothing to do with the question.

A woman who believes that she has a right to an abortion, which should require no further justification than that she wants it, as an instance of her right to self-determination (the 'it's-my-body' argument) overlooks morally important aspects of her own situation.

THE MORAL ISSUE

The embryo or fetus, while it is indubitably in her body, is not hers alone. It is not just a tissue of her body as, say, an excisable blemish on her skin would be. Even in these days of reproductive wonders, of cloning and the not-distant possibility of parthenogenesis for example, the fetus or embryo is still the product of the fusion of two gametes, the male and female. Moreover, even nowadays, when reproduction has been divorced from sex in the way that a few years ago sex was divorced from reproduction, the great majority of children are conceived in the traditional fashion, by means of sexual intercourse between a man and a woman. Though it is true that the woman carries all the physical and most of the psychological burdens of gestation, it still cannot and ought not to be said that the biological father of the child she carries has or should have no interest in the outcome of the pregnancy. The offspring is as much his as it is hers, at least genetically speaking; and if it is reasonable, as I believe it to be, that the biological father of a child is held to have inescapable responsibilities, financial and otherwise, towards that child, he can hardly be treated as if his opinion as to the continuation or termination of a pregnancy is of no account or moral significance whatsoever: which it would be, if the woman's supposed right to self-determination were the only principle that had to be taken into account in making the decision.

Of course, as I know from my own clinical experience, increasing numbers of women are choosing to have children by men about whose qualities they care nothing, and who are self-evidently not going to support their offspring in any way. This trend is itself a reflection of the influence of the doctrine of rights, inasmuch as the women believe themselves to have a right to a child: not merely in the negative sense that it is not the business of the Government to determine who may and may not bear children, but in the sense that if they want a child, then not to have one is an infringement of that to which they are morally entitled. Their ability to support a child, or the quality of the life they can offer that child (often terrible beyond my powers to describe it) simply does not merit a moment's consideration, as far as they are concerned. A right is not a right if it is hedged round by restrictions or curtailed by qualifications of any kind. Clearly, the negligent and irresponsible fathers of the children of such mothers can hardly lay a moral claim to a say in the question of whether their unborn child should be aborted: though often in practice they do so nonetheless, by means of physical violence, either kicking the woman in the stomach to procure an abortion when she wants to continue with the pregnancy, or beating her up when she has had an abortion of which he disapproves.

Where, however, the pregnancy is the outcome of a more stable and loving relationship between a man and a woman, and where the man would assume the duties of a father if the child were born, it is clear that the woman is not morally entitled to treat the embryo or fetus in her uterus as purely her own, of no concern to anyone else. However, when it comes to the question of whether or not to abort, votes cannot be distributed as if the relationship between the mother and the father were a joint stock company, each having a certain number of votes according to their original and continuing investment in the offspring. Civilized people simply do not make decisions about intimate matters in this way: they do not consider their rights at all.

That the operation of abortion itself is different, morally speaking, from other operations is attested by the fact that most (though by no means all) women who undergo it recognize its difference from all other operations. It is not for them just the removal of a pathological blot in their body, akin to a cholecystectomy. Indeed, if it were, the moral question concerning its permissibility would hardly have arisen in the first place. No one agonizes over the ethics of the removal of a tumour or the relief of an obstructed bowel.

Of what, then, does the difference between abortion and other operations consist? It is surely its obvious connection with the ultimate and most fundamental value of human existence: a connection that the amputation of a limb, serious as it may be, does not have. If human life is to have any meaning at all, it must be treated religiously, as sacred, even by those without a conventional faith in God. The problem with abortion is that it treats human life instrumentally, and not as sacred, as if human life (and an embryo or fetus is human life, even if it is not yet a full person) were merely a means to procure some other advantage, like happiness, prestige or contentment. If every decision in human life is treated as a mere utilitarian calculation, a horrible shallowness results. And it is probably no coincidence that in an age of abortion, so many children are born not as the expression of two people's belief in the intrinsic value of human life, which they therefore wish to continue, but as virtual fashion accessories, to be shown off to others as an achievement (usually only during infancy, whereafter the offspring become a drain on resources and a tiresome nuisance in all other respects), or as the solution to a personal problem ('I thought a baby would be someone to love who would love me back,' as so many mothers have pathetically told me). Where human life itself is treated instrumentally, the most trivial of reasons is considered sufficient reason to end it: the mother does not wish to risk morning sickness during a forthcoming holiday to Spain, for example. But it is precisely because so many women realize that human life ought not to be treated in this fashion that they experience abortion as traumatic, in a deep philosophical sense, in a way that other operations are not experienced as traumatic.

The law, however, is necessarily coarse-grained, far more so than life. It has to state what is and what is not permissible, and every eventuality cannot be legislated for (which is why private virtue is so necessary, even, or perhaps especially, in a free society). It must either permit or forbid abortion: and if the former, it must state under what conditions. Because these conditions could not possibly be described exhaustively, with every human eventuality catered for, and therefore any law (that permitted rather than altogether proscribed abortion) would have to leave certain matters to the discretion of women and their doctors.

The original Abortion Act in Great Britain did precisely this. It was never intended to be a law to permit abortion on demand, though this is what it has, *de facto*, become. It is very unlikely that any British woman in the past few years has been denied an abortion on the grounds that she does not fulfil the criteria laid down in the Act: though of course it is equally unlikely that all of those who had abortions did in fact fulfil the criteria. Parliament intended abortion to be a medical procedure of last resort, a relief of severe and otherwise unavoidable suffering, for example, in the case of a 12-year-old girl who had been raped.

Why has the drift occurred? In large part it is because of the cowardice of doctors, who have lost the stomach to deny their patients anything they want. Their patients have increasingly come to think of themselves as customers, indeed have been encouraged to do so, and now become annoyed and querulous – as thwarted shoppers do – when the shopkeeper-doctor tells them that he does not have what they want. Permission for abortions is granted to avoid the unpleasant scenes that a more rigorous interpretation of the law would occasion. At the same time, however, people who are granted what they believe they have a right to are not satisfied by it, for two reasons: first because no one is grateful for the receipt of what he is entitled to (for if he were grateful, it would not be an entitlement), and second because people invoke their rights and entitlements mainly when they know that what they are demanding is morally wrong. That is why abortion can be demanded as an entitlement, as a subsidiary right to the right of personal autonomy and self-determination, and yet be acknowledged to be different in kind from other medical procedures. The conflict between the attitudes leads to a deep existential unease.

CONCLUSION

Is there any prospect of permitting abortion without permitting abortion on demand? I very much doubt it. People these days are reluctant to submit themselves to external sources of moral authority, which they consider inherently illegitimate (though without which life is a torment, for each person is then left to decide everything for himself, the desire of the moment being the sole criterion by which to make the decision). What right, asks modern man, has anyone to tell me how I should organize my life? In other words, in the reigning cultural climate, it will be very difficult to achieve with regard to abortion a respect for the general sanctity of human life while at the same time recognizing that abortion is, in some circumstances, humane. The crudity of modern moral discourse, in which ignorant armies clash by night, prevents the necessary subtle distinctions from being made.

44

Essay Four

ABORTION IS A FACT OF LIFE
Ann Furedi

Every year the publication of the annual abortion statistics provokes a discussion about why Britain's abortion rate remains high relative to other European countries. Every year, sexual health experts express disappointment that the increased efforts and resources directed at sex education and contraceptive services seem to have had marginal impact on the number of women who need to end unwanted pregnancies.

Those who oppose legal abortion insist that the abortion rate is a symptom of a 'culture of convenience' and a 'degraded out-of-control society'. In truth, it may be that the British abortion rate is evidence that women have a strong desire to keep control of their lives. It may be that many women, realizing that there is more to life than motherhood, are not prepared to let an unplanned and unwanted pregnancy shape their destiny. It may be that, for many women in modern Britain, abortion is seen as the solution to a problem rather than a problem in itself. Perhaps it is time to conclude that abortion has become as much a part of contemporary life as e-mail, espresso and Lycra.

ABORTION AS A METHOD OF FAMILY PLANNING

In 2001, almost 200,000 women resident in Britain experienced an abortion. In the last decade the proportion of women throughout the fertile age range who take advantage of safe legal abortion has risen significantly. In 1991, 15 women in every thousand requested and obtained an abortion, by 2001 the figure had increased to almost 17 – a significant rise in just a decade. For women in their early twenties the abortion rate increased from 27 per thousand to 30. Four women in every ten experience abortion at some point in their reproductive life, making it one of the most common surgical procedures.

There are many reasons why the number of abortions continues to rise. Over the last 20 years many of the fluctuations in the abortion rate have reflected changes in the population. However, the recent increase is not simply a matter of demography. Throughout the 1980s increased numbers of abortions were due largely to an increased number of fertile women in the population – as the 1960s baby boom generation reached reproductive age. From 1990 to 1995 the rate of abortions slowly but surely fell. When the trend reversed in 1996, and the abortion rate shot up, there seemed to be an obvious explanation. In October 1995, the safety of the contraceptive pill was questioned in a manner that led to one of the biggest ever health panics. In response to health warnings about the risk of thrombosis, tens of thousands of women needlessly abandoned their preferred method of contraceptive. It was no surprise that thousands of unplanned, unintended pregnancies were the result – and it was no surprise that many of these ended in abortion. In 1996 the number of abortions rose by nine per cent on the previous year, and the increase attracted a huge amount of publicity. Previous contraceptive scares had had similar effects, but in the case of previous scares, the abortion rate had risen and then gradually returned to the *status quo ante* as women drifted back to using the Pill. The shared assumption that this would happen again has turned out to be false.

It may be that the 1995 Pill scare, and the publicity surrounding the abortion aftermath, placed in the minds of women what had hitherto been unspoken: that abortion was a safe and legal option in the case of unwanted pregnancy. Abortion became positioned as a method of fertility regulation – a second chance when contraception failed.

Policy makers are reluctant to admit that abortion has been accepted as a method of family planning. Even those who are pro-choice are hesitant to define it in these terms. Abortion is still seen as a 'necessary evil', something that many in the pro-choice movement insist must be 'safe, legal and rare'. Abortion is usually perceived as 'a problem': something that liberals hope to eliminate through better use of contraception, and conservatives hope to address through confining sex to the marriage bed. Often, arguments for increased access to contraception and for new contraceptive technologies are built on the assumption that these developments will bring down the abortion rate. The anti-choice movement counter that this does not seem to be the case in practice. Arguably they are right. Access to effective contraception creates an expectation that women can control their fertility and plan their families. Given that expectation, women may be less willing to compromise their plans for the future. In the past, many women reluctantly accepted that an unplanned pregnancy would lead to maternity. Unwanted pregnancies were dutifully, if resentfully, carried to term. In days when sex was expected to carry the risk of pregnancy, an unwanted child was a chance a woman took. Today, we expect sex to be free from that risk and unplanned maternity is not a price we are prepared to pay.

It is clear that women cannot manage their fertility by means of contraception alone. Contraception lets couples down. A recent survey of more than 2,000 women requesting abortion at clinics run by BPAS, Britain's largest abortion provider, found that almost 60 per cent claimed to have been using contraception at the time they became pregnant. Nearly 20 per cent said they were on the Pill. Such findings are comparable to several other smaller studies published during the last decade. The number of women who claim they experienced a split or slipped condom, or missed just a couple of pills, is undoubtedly inflated. Unprotected sex is highly stigmatized and some women may falsely claim to have used contraception believing that they will be treated more sympathetically if people believe they did everything possible to prevent the pregnancy. Nevertheless, it is clear that contraceptives let couples down. Whether the pregnancy occurred because the condom split or because the couple failed to get it out of the packet is of less importance to a woman needing an abortion than it is to family planning professionals who debate whether unplanned pregnancy is due to contraceptive 'method failure' or 'user failure'. The simple truth is that the tens of thousands of women who seek abortion each year are not ignorant of contraception. Rather they have tried to use it, indeed they may have used it, and become pregnant regardless.

Society has tacitly come to accept that abortion has come to be used as a method of family planning, if by that we mean that women use abortion to control whether or when they have children. That is not to say that people are indifferent to whether a pregnancy is started or ended. Most women find abortion upsetting and distressing and would rather avoid the need for one. However, in contemporary Britain – at least among middle-class women – fertility control has come to be seen as a spectrum of methods. Routine, regular contraception usually prevents an egg from being fertilized. Post-coital contraception (and some regular methods such as IUDs) may prevent a fertilized egg from implanting, and so prevent a pregnancy from being established. Early medical abortion causes the pregnant uterus to expel the developing embryo. Later methods of abortion remove a fetus. While most women would prefer to prevent fertilization – most are prepared to accept post-fertilization intervention when necessary.

However, it would be wrong to claim contraceptive failure is an adequate explanation for an elevated abortion rate. It is inconceivable that contraception is less reliable now than it was 25 years ago, when the abortion rate was almost half that of today. Rather, it is more likely that in the past women were more likely to accept and continue an unwanted pregnancy in times when they were expected, and expected themselves, to have a 'job' rather than a 'career' and a 'husband' rather than a 'partner'. Today women experience pregnancy in a very different context.

◆ ● ● THE PLACE OF ABORTION IN WOMEN'S LIVES TODAY

The increase in women's recourse to abortion should be understood alongside other changes in society that may make women less likely to accept unintended motherhood. Women today are far more likely to cohabit with a lover throughout their twenties than they are to get married. This is important because marriage seems to be one of the most significant influences on a woman's acceptance of an unplanned pregnancy, probably because the act of getting married represents stability and a commitment to the future. Cohabiting women, when they get pregnant, seem to act more like single women than married women. Just 17 per cent of conceptions to married women end in abortions compared with more than 40 per cent of conceptions to single women.

More women are deciding to reject motherhood altogether, and national statistics show that those women who do have children want to have fewer of them, later in life. Currently, one woman in five is childless at 40. Some of these women will have experienced fertility problems, but a far greater proportion regard itself as 'childfree'. The increase in the average age of first birth in 2000 to almost 30 years of age suggests that a great many women are highly motivated to avoid pregnancy during the fertile twenty-something years. When children are clearly not on a woman's personal agenda, it is hardly surprising that abortion is seen as a sensible means of managing a problem pregnancy.

Such changes in women's lives are arguably reflected in increased public tolerance of abortion, and the marginalization of anti-choice views has been demonstrated by recent surveys of public opinion, most notably a MORI poll conducted in October 2001. This survey of a statistically representative sample of 2000 adults found that about two-thirds (65 per cent) agreed that if a woman wanted an abortion she should not have to continue with an unwanted pregnancy, just one person in six disagreed. The proportion of people who approved of abortion when a woman did not want to have a child increased from 42 per cent, when the same question was asked in 1997, to 50 per cent.

The poll revealed that social background has a significant influence on attitude to abortion. Social classes ABC1 are more likely to agree than C2DEs that women who want an abortion should not have to continue their pregnancy (70 per cent compared with 60 per cent). Those who read broadsheet papers are more likely to agree than those who read tabloids (73 per cent compared with 64 per cent). And those with most qualifications are more inclined to agree (74 per cent of those with A levels or the equivalent agree compared with 57 per cent of those with no formal qualifications). Reproductive choice, it seems, is most highly valued by those with the capacity to exercise choice in other areas of their lives.

Attitudes to abortion exist as part of a web of other ideas that interface with social values on other issues such as poverty, perceptions of women's role in society, the value of parenting and even global issues such as the environment and over-population. There is a general acceptance throughout most Western societies that women should expect, and be expected, to make a broader contribution to society than solely devoting their life to bearing and caring for the next generation. Motherhood is still regarded as 'natural' at some time in a woman's life, but most people assume that motherhood will be an interval sandwiched on both sides by an income-generating 'job' if not a 'career'. Girls from appropriate (middle-class) backgrounds are expected to progress to a university education.

Increased tolerance of abortion may also reflect a society that places a high premium on *planned* parenthood. There is a strong prevailing belief that children should be wanted and that parents should be able to support them and be willing to make sacrifices for them. Growing social concern about 'unfit' or 'problem' parents does not easily co-exist with a disposition to force people to bear children they do not want and by their own admission cannot care for. This ethos creates a framework whereby even social conservatives who would disapprove of abortion in principle can in some circumstances perceive abortion as a 'responsible choice'.

The general acceptance of abortion has allowed policy makers to place abortion on the reproductive health care agenda. Even in the early 1990s, the 'A' word was almost entirely absent from health policy documents. By 2001, government was sufficiently comfortable with the issue to publish a sexual health strategy that included specific targets for the improvement of abortion services. It also pledged to commit to fund publicly procedures for women who meet the legal requirements for abortion. Ministers would still prefer to avoid debate on abortion in Parliament, but there seems to be a consensus among policy makers that it should be provided effectively and efficiently as an integral part of reproductive health care. Opponents of legal abortion have protested that this will make it easier for women to terminate their pregnancies. And why should it not be made easier? There is no evidence to suggest that the safe legal abortions provided in Britain's hospitals and specialist clinics pose a risk to women's health. There is no evidence to suggest that it causes lasting physical or psychological damage. The social and economic cost of abortion is likely to be less than that of forcing women into unwilling motherhood. There are no compelling reasons to restrict women's access to abortion if the procedure is understood to be legal and legitimate – and in Britain today clearly it is.

A MATTER OF PRINCIPLE

So, abortion is now accepted and acceptable. But it remains stigmatized. Abortion is seen as a 'necessary evil', a moral 'wrong', a bad act that can sometimes be justified by good reasons. Society is schizophrenic in its approach striving to reconcile two distinct but related sets of considerations. There are 'moral–ethical' considerations and there are 'practical–pragmatic' considerations. The ethical discussion continues to problematize abortion, perceiving it to be an abstract, moral wrong that should be minimized. The practical–pragmatic discussion is shaped by the weight of evidence presented above – that unwanted pregnancies occur, that they are a problem for women, and abortion is an appropriate solution.

In so far as it can be said that pro-choice opinions hold sway, it is a pro-choiceness of pragmatic solutions to problems rather than pro-choiceness of principle that has come to dominate. Abortion is accepted because the alternative, forcing resentful women into motherhood, is seen to be worse. The principle of reproductive autonomy, that women should be able to obtain abortions because no one should deny them the right to make that decision about their own pregnancy, has not been won. Arguably, it has not been won because it has not been fought for. The gradual acceptance of abortion by default, with policy following the practice of women and doctors rather than determining that practice, has been hugely convenient for women, the medical profession and policy makers. It has allowed the evolution of abortion on request, a prerequisite of a society that seeks to integrate women into public life, with relatively little controversy. It would now seem bizarre to turn back the clock and insist that a woman who forgot to take her contraceptive pill 'face the consequences' and have the resulting child.

However, pro-choice pragmatism is not as robust as pro-choice principle, and it may be that women's current degree of access to abortion is vulnerable because of this. It is unlikely that there will be an assault on the principle that abortion should be available as a back-up to contraception – but just as it has been allowed for pragmatic reasons, it may come to be restricted for pragmatic reasons. For example, discussion constantly rumbles about the acceptability of the time limit for abortion. With a limit of 24 weeks in most circumstances (and a few exceptions when there is no upper time limit), Britain allows abortions at more advanced gestations than almost any other country. It is often argued that developments in neo-natal medicine allow babies that are born at gestations lower than the abortion rate to survive and live to enjoy a reasonable quality of life. Most doctors, even those who specialize in abortion, find the techniques involved in late abortions unpleasant. And later abortions are far more costly to provide, meaning that there is a disincentive for clinics to maintain this part of their service.

The pragmatic case for reducing the time limit on abortion is already being rehearsed, and may well obtain public support. The idea of a woman taking drugs to induce the miscarriage of products of conception the size of a pea is far more acceptable to the public mind than the destruction of a fetus that resembles a tiny baby. Ultimately, the request of a woman for an abortion in late pregnancy can only be sustained by the principled argument that she must make the decision, according to her conscience, because she will live with the consequences for the rest of her life.

The pragmatic extension of abortion is also problematic in that it has left the legal framework established in 1967 intact. This means that, according to the law, a woman cannot make a choice to end her pregnancy. Abortion remains illegal unless two doctors agree that she is, essentially, unfit to be a mother because continuing the pregnancy will cause damage to her physical or mental health, or to that of other children in the family. The law may be interpreted liberally, and it is. Social factors, such as poverty, may be taken into consideration. In some ways, the abortion law stands as a model law – strict enough to regulate, but drafted flexibly enough to allow changing interpretations. On paper, the law is one of the strictest in Europe; in practice it is one of the most liberal. Yet, the very existence of this law, and the fact that women have to obtain confirmation from doctors that they meet the specified legal requirements, means that women seeking abortion are degraded and positioned as victims. Women are made to play a game. The ambitious professional woman who wishes to end her pregnancy because it will jeopardize her promotion is forced to pretend she is incapable of coping emotionally or physically with a child, and her doctor pretends to believe her. This situation undermines, and is degrading to, both doctors and women. Furthermore, it perpetuates a dishonest view that abortion is performed because of medical indications when the truth is that in most circumstances abortion is requested because a woman does not want a child and not because she would be an unfit mother.

The pragmatic acceptance of abortion by society and the state, may also lead to the *promotion* of abortion on pragmatic grounds. Government policy to address the issue of teenage pregnancy contains an implicit assumption that, whilst it would be better for girls not to get pregnant, if they do abortion is preferable to teenage motherhood. This is unproblematic in the case of young girls for whom pregnancy is a mistake that they quickly want to correct. It may well raise problems for young girls who are opposed to abortion, or who have conceived because they want a child. The social exclusion of teenage mothers is a genuine social problem but, if we support abortion out of respect for the reproductive autonomy of women, we cannot encourage it as an eugenic solution to social exclusion or poverty.

Because the moral argument against abortion has not been defeated, and the argument for procreative autonomy has not been won, the parameters of the debate have shifted. Anti-choice groups, understanding that the weight of public opinion and social practice was against them, have almost ceased any active campaign against the early abortion that accounts for 98 per cent of pregnancy terminations. They have conceded to the pragmatic acceptance of abortion for unwanted pregnancy and understand that their favoured alternative option of adoption is unacceptable to the public at large. However, they have simply refocused their arguments onto those issues where the politics of pragmatism cannot so easily defeat them – specifically in relation to research on embryos, and euthanasia. These are issues where their perspective is less marginal – even though many of the intellectual tenets are those that they would employ in challenging abortion.

The creeping acceptance of abortion on pragmatic grounds – that it is needed as a back-up to contraception if society is to function – has stripped the debate of its moral content. The discourse has, in effect, been 'de-moralized'. Discussions of principle have been by-passed. This has resulted in some gains for women. Abortion in Britain is, in effect, available on request, despite the seemingly restrictive legislation. But it has left the argument about the moral appropriateness of abortion hanging in the air.

Abortion, although widely available, remains stigmatized and perceived as 'a wrong' – even if it is the right choice for a particular circumstance. Women choose abortion because they wish to take back control of their lives and maintain their independence, but their decision is often characterized as selfish or immature. Abortion is a part of our lives – but it remains shameful. Women often feel the need to apologize for terminating a pregnancy – as though there is something wrong. Policy makers feel the need to 'regret' the relatively high abortion rate – as though there is something wrong.

CONCLUSION

Most people have accepted that abortion is a fact of modern life. It would be better if we could accept that abortion is a *legitimate* fact of modern life and that it can be a mature, responsible and moral decision. In his thoughtful exploration of the ethics of life and death, *Life's Dominion: an argument about abortion and euthanasia* (1993), legal scholar Ronald Dworkin argues that the most important feature of our culture is a belief in individual human dignity. Central to human dignity, he argues, is the principle 'that people have the moral right – and the moral responsibility – to confront the most fundamental questions about the value and meaning of their own lives for themselves, answering to their own consciences and convictions'. This is particularly relevant to decisions about reproduction. A civilized society accepts that women are creatures with a moral conscience who are capable of making responsible decisions for themselves. That is a principle British society has yet to accept.

Pragmatically, society accepts that women need access to abortion. Now we need to shift to an argument of principle. Abortion can be a responsible, moral choice. Perhaps the most fundamental argument to be had is whether women can be trusted to make responsible ethical decisions and considered choices. Until that issue is resolved in their favour, women's continued access to abortion remains insecure.

CHOICES, RIGHTS AND PARADOXES IN THE ABORTION STORY
Mary Kenny

There have been many compelling cases of women desperate to terminate a pregnancy, and many odd cases too. I remember receiving a letter from a woman who said that pregnancy gave her a most frightful feeling of being imprisoned in her own body; the whole experience was a nightmare because she felt she was being taken over by an alien growing within her, and she could not rest until she had terminated the pregnancy. (The 1979 Ridley Scott movie *Alien*, when a dreadful creature bursts forth from John Hurt's stomach, was a visualization of the phobic fear in question.) Later, this woman conceived again, and again the feeling of being imprisoned obsessed her, and she felt obliged, once more, to terminate.

Recently, this condition has been diagnosed as 'tokophobia' – a pathological fear of childbirth, and the National Phobics Society takes an average of five calls a week from women with such a phobic fear. Simone de Beauvoir, in *The Second Sex*, wrote about pregnancy in mildly phobic terms, describing how a woman who felt formerly autonomous becomes, once pregnant, simply 'the plaything of nature': perhaps these feelings contributed to de Beauvoir's own decision to choose abortion, at least twice, rather than bear a child with Sartre.

Two very sad cases that I encountered involved terminating a pregnancy as a reaction to grief. In one case a woman in her thirties became pregnant with her second child, and was quite happy about it. Then, tragically, her first child was killed in an accident. She was so distressed about losing her son that she insisted on terminating the second pregnancy, saying that she could not abide to have another child now. She duly had an abortion, and never had any more children. When widowed later in life, quixotically, she became a Roman Catholic, and somehow found in faith an answer and a meaning to her tragedy.

The second case I encountered was where a woman had an abortion at 23 weeks – on the cusp of infant viability – because she had lost her fiancé in a car crash. She said that she did not want to have a child that would remind her of her dead sweetheart. This seems an atypical reaction to loss – more women would, I think, want to continue the pregnancy for that very reason: many people empathized with Diane Blood, who fought for the right (denied in Britain, granted in Belgium) to conceive a child from her dead husband's sperm. But there is no accounting for folks, and this was how this particular woman reacted to her loss. Whether the termination at 23 weeks for this reason is ethical medicine may be a subject of dispute: I certainly encountered more than one feminist philosopher who did not believe that 'the right to choose' extends to the point of possible infant viability, and that by 23 weeks, an unborn child has acquired rights which can be swept aside only for urgent medical reasons.

But then, as Dr Bernard Nathanson has said in his poignant and even witty memoir as a semi-legal abortionist *Aborting America* (1979), women will seek abortions as late as they can go. He describes receiving requests for the termination of pregnancy at eight months gestation. There are known cases of such very late abortions: the writer Anais Nin had an abortion when the fetus was apparently alive, and there was a celebrated actress in the 1940s who aborted at almost eight months. Does 'the right to choose' have limits? Yes, since that is the reason why laws exist which make it illegal to abort a child beyond a certain gestation (in Britain this is when the child 'is capable of being born alive', which is around 23–24 weeks pregnancy. Most countries in Europe have earlier deadlines.)

However, if 'the right to choose' has a limit, it is therefore only a limited right. It thus cannot be an absolute right. This is one of the reasons why abortion remains contentious and why there will always be wide differences of opinion about its 'rightness', both in the moral and in the entitlement sense of the word.

 **MIXED FEELINGS**

The terms of the discourse about abortion have changed and shifted over the past 35 years. In the 1960s, the drive to legalize abortion was posited strongly upon the hard cases of backstreet abortions, which did indeed exist, although by 1963 death from illegal abortion was reduced to virtually zero, partly because of antibiotics and partly because 'illegal' abortion was *de facto* becoming legal and medicalized. Case law had established that it was permissible for a doctor to terminate a pregnancy if, in good faith, he believed it was necessary for his patient, and by the early 1960s this was being more widely interpreted. But there were still obstacles to obtaining an abortion – you had to know a willing doctor, have a good network, be in the appropriate place (Oxford was practising legal abortion by 1963) and generally have the available cash – and there still remained some dangerous and illegal abortions carried out in back parlours.

Anna Raeburn has spoken with characteristic passion and distress, in Gina Newson's 1984 Channel 4 documentary 'Mixed Feelings' (also published in book form in 1986), about the illegal abortion which she underwent in the early 1960s, which involved a medical student squirting washing-up liquid into her vagina. The French writer Annie Ernaux has written a compelling but dismal autobiographical essay L'Evenement (2000) about her wretched abortion as a student in Paris in the 1960s, the entire operation carried out in secrecy and silence.

Such experiences convinced many women of that generation, coming of age in the 1960s, that the termination of pregnancy must be legalized and, unsurprisingly, the illegal and the dangerous backstreet abortion was the focus of the reformers' campaigns previous to the passing of the controversial Abortion Act of 1967, which came into law in April 1968. It was perhaps paradoxical that the era of the contraceptive Pill – which had been made available in Britain in 1961 – and which had been hailed as an innovation that would halt all unwanted pregnancies forever, also heralded legalized abortion. But not as paradoxical as it might seem.

The contraceptive Pill was a very effective means of birth control – in laboratory circumstances. Human use was something else: you could forget it, you could get fed up with it when it made you fat, you could quit taking it when you broke up with your boyfriend, only to fall into bed spontaneously with someone else: you could get drunk and vomit it up, a not at all unusual circumstance then, or indeed now. But the contraceptive Pill gradually created a new sexual climate and new expectations about a woman's right to control her body. Abortion became more acceptable as a *result* of better contraception, since it gradually seemed to assume the guise of 'retrospective contraception'. 'We offer an abortion service as a chance to put the clock back' a young counsellor told me brightly at the Marie Stopes Clinic during the course of my own research. A pregnancy commenced, once regarded as a dramatic and virtually irrevocable change in a woman's life, could now be undone.

I remember hearing a conversation between two Irish women during the 1970s, in which one was telling the other that she was pregnant for the fifth time. Commiserations were expressed and exchanged, and the pregnant one sighed: 'I need a fifth child like a hole in the head but, sure, what can I do about it now? What's done is done'. Indeed, her friend agreed, she'd have to accept and make the best of it. I said nothing, but I remember thinking, 'Oh yes, there is something you can do about it; you don't have to accept passively what you have not chosen.' I was new woman whose mental formation had been changed by the era of the Pill and the easy availability of abortion in London – and of course by the feminism linked to it. Whereas they were traditional women, 'archaic' in my view, formed by the native Roman Catholicism whose most insistent image is the Blessed Virgin Mary at The Annunciation – that most painted subject in European art – bowing her head and 'accepting' the child an Angel had announced to her.

Thirty years on, the pregnancy grumbled about between the two women is a radiant and beautiful young woman herself, a brilliant lawyer and an adored daughter. An unwillingly pregnancy does not always turn into an unwanted child and a chosen abortion does not necessarily guarantee lifelong satisfaction. Thirty years on I see women who I know chose to terminate pregnancies because they did not want children at that time, and I sometimes glimpse that *kinderlostraurig* the Germans speak of – 'the sadness of childlessness' – in their countenance. The clock does not go back: the moving finger writes, and having writ, moves on.

A MATTER OF CHOICE?

Immediately following the 1967 Abortion Act, the birth rate did indeed begin to drop (the number of babies available for adoption zoomed downwards almost overnight), and gradually more women began to use abortion – not for the hard case agenda that had been so piteously sketched, but as a matter of choice. 'Choice' became the buzz-word of the feminist and post-feminist eras, and 'the right to choose' one of the most persuasive and successful slogans of all time. 'Choice' covered all eventualities and at all times: it was launched by the Left ('The Right to Choose' was first coined by a British feminist and Communist Stella Browne in 1915 writing in *The Malthusian*). But it was also much favoured by the free market philosophy which was to have such a revival in the 1980s under Thatcher and Reagan. Some Christians, even some Catholics, have argued that 'choice' is four-square in the Christian tradition of free will. The Catholic Church is insistent that the contract of marriage must be undertaken voluntarily, and therefore must be one of free choice; coercion has been, for many centuries, grounds for the annulment of marriage. 'Choice' is a concept of high pedigree, and it has spread well beyond the sphere of abortion; in many fields it has improved the quality of life and, even arguably, the sense of responsibility. If you have freely chosen a course of action, then you are much more responsible for what follows.

Choice had a profound effect on medical approaches to patient care. Immediately up to, and after, the legalization of abortion in the United Kingdom, doctors in general retained their own personal attitudes to abortion. Some would, some would not, some would in certain circumstances, but not in others. Gradually over the next decades this altered to patient choice, even if a few doctors (and nurses) have retained a conscientious objection to carrying out terminations of pregnancy, usually on religious grounds.

Few gynaecologists have explained this change better than the late Professor Peter Huntingford, a maverick, eccentric but not unlikeable gynaecologist, who switched from being an Evangelical Christian converted by Billy Graham to a driven radical who declared wildly that he would perform an abortion on any woman, at any point in the pregnancy, and for any reason.

Huntingford had an anguished attitude to abortion when he began practising as a gynaecologist in the early 1960s. He did not favour termination of pregnancy but he did agree to do some special cases. He was working at a London teaching hospital where there would be a committee meeting to discuss 'hard cases': which abortions might be carried out, and which might be refused. Two particular incidents, running together, completely altered his outlook. In case one, a married woman with a large family sought an abortion because her circumstances were financially straitened and her husband had just been sent to jail. She said she simply could not face having another child and was feeling suicidal. In case two, a young schoolgirl of just 16 was pregnant after 'going too far' with her boyfriend – that is, the girl had not intended to have full sexual intercourse, but it had happened.

Peter Huntingford judged that the overburdened married mother with the large family and poor housing should be permitted to terminate her pregnancy because of her circumstances; whereas the schoolgirl should face the consequences of her actions and have the child. A year later, he had reason to revisit these cases when the married woman returned to see him, saying she was pregnant again, and now wanted to have the baby. 'But last year you said you couldn't possibly go through another pregnancy!' he said. 'Oh well,' she smiled. 'I sort of got a second wind'. Peter Huntingford made enquiries about the fate of the schoolgirl and found that she had been devastated by having a baby at 16, had been unable to cope with it, and had been suffused by grief in putting it up for adoption. At that moment, he told me at interview, he decided he would never again sit in judgement of a woman seeking to terminate a pregnancy. It was up to the woman to choose, he decided. As for doctors, they should agree to all abortions, or to none: it was the only consistent position. He decided to do all, and went to some melodramatic extremes in upholding that policy. Yet he too was prey to mixed feelings. He summed up the conflicting rights of the unborn child and the woman thus: 'The fetus has a right to life. But only the mother can protect that right.'

◆●● ●● ●●◆ A NEW MORAL ORDER

Thus, as the last decades of the twentieth century passed, abortion gradually became accepted as a choice, although some people could never see it as an ethical choice. The Roman Catholic Church, broadly though less vehemently backed by other Christians and by some Jews, refused to alter its moral condemnation of abortion in all circumstances, staunchly maintaining that human life began at conception, and it could never be right deliberately to kill the unborn in the womb. It also maintained – though less staunchly at least at grass-roots level – its opposition to 'artificial' contraception, as outlined in the Papal Encyclical of 1968, *Humanae Vitae*. Liberal Catholics were appalled at Pope Paul VI's decision, against many of his own advisers, to anathematize contraception and it provoked a crisis within the Church. Contraception, many argued, was necessary not just as responsible family planning for young couples who could not afford to have too many babies, but as a hedge against abortion.

Logically it seemed that way but in practice *Humanae Vitae* turned out to be objectively correct in many respects. Contraception did not prevent abortion, but merged with it. Birth control did not preserve marriage (as Marie Stopes said it would), but provided more freedom of choice for divorce. And once the link between the sexual act and 'the transmission of life' was broken, the natural law would indeed be put aside and all kinds of doubtful innovations would follow. The sex act is no longer necessarily associated with the making of babies, and married heterosexual intercourse now claims no privileges over any other kind of sexuality. The making of babies through a bewildering variety of routes, from IVF to cloning, proceeds apace because the link has been broken between conjugality and procreation. Mr Hugh Hefner proved to be the prophet of the age when he announced that from the onset of the Pill, sex would be about 'recreation, not procreation'.

The role of the Catholic Church is significant in its world-wide opposition to abortion. Where abortion law reform is planned, opposition can generally be expected from The Holy See. I am myself a practising Catholic and I admire and support the Church's valiant and consistent defence of the unborn child through thick and thin: it is not easy to be completely out of step with the spirit of the age and to oppose a reform which country after country in the developed world, and elsewhere too, has gradually embraced. Catholics have been described as misogynists, gender-fascists, oppressors and much more because of this stance, and individual Catholics have suffered in their careers – certainly in medicine – because of their moral view of abortion. Virtually all boards, committees and trusts enquiring into the ethics of reproduction now exclude Catholics from their number, for fear of their opposition – and because there is a great fear of open debate on contentious issues. Quangos like to appoint yes-men, and yes-women: they want consensus, not the dialectic of debate.

However, even the Catholic Church, with all its opposition to abortion, has been affected by abortion law reform. It has had to develop a sharper analysis of rights and rights-based ideas: where once the Magisterium, the teaching authority of the Church, abhorred the notion of 'rights' as a devilish French Revolutionary notion, it has now embraced the notion of rights as much as any Jacobin revolutionary, because it affirms the right of the unborn child not to be killed. Moreover, social attitudes have changed greatly within the Catholic value system because of the shifts wrought by abortion law reform. Whereas the unmarried mother, previously, would have been stigmatized for her sin (and where it was possible to apply social pressure the unmarried father would be pressed into a shotgun marriage) now the unmarried mother is accepted as a good girl who has not had an abortion. Indeed, the late Cardinal Winning of Scotland went so far as to pay young girls to become unmarried mothers, rather than see them terminate a pregnancy. More attention has been given to the health of mothers, to promoting breast-feeding particularly in poor countries, and even to discussing 'choice' in the arena of fertility awareness.

At the UN Women's Conference held at Beijing in 1995, I attended an electrifying workshop run by Catholics on natural family planning, where women from all over the globe spoke with eloquence on the theme of their relationship to their own body which natural fertility awareness had helped to explore. The Quebecois Catholic leading the discussion started out by emphasizing the choices and even the autonomy proceeding from natural fertility theory. The language of abortion rights has undoubtedly seeped into places formerly presided over by abortion's fiercest opponents.

The question of regarding all human life as part of the Incarnation – the divine in the human – has also provoked more liberal thinking in Catholic moral philosophy on matters of war and the death penalty. Pope John Paul II has become a passionate opponent of the death penalty, and a Catholic nun Sister Helen Prejean (played by Susan Sarandon in the 1995 movie *Dead Man Walking*), has become the world's most celebrated witness at Death Row. Thinking about abortion rights and wrongs has also helped to develop a moral philosophy on euthanasia, another extremely difficult area of 'life rights'.

The French feminist Francoise Giraud once said that the Pill affected everyone, whether they took it or not, since it affected the *idea* of controlling one's fertility. Abortion rights have similarly affected everyone, whether they agree with abortion or not. And even though I uphold the orthodox Catholic position on abortion, I would say that the notion of abortion rights has helped to produce, by the way, some good outcomes. Fertility control in general has given women a greater sense of confidence in themselves, and the idea of choice in continuing a pregnancy has, paradoxically, also helped some women to make the choice to *have* the baby. During my interviews with women who recall the pre-1960s period, some of the saddest instances were those of women who had had secret abortions they would not have wanted, had there been real choice. I remember a Scandinavian diplomat, who fell in love with an African colleague: she conceived a child, but felt, at that time, that for a single woman in the diplomatic service to bear a mixed-race child would have been professionally unacceptable. Mournfully, she terminated the pregnancy, and mourned that child for many years. Today, a woman in that position would, I think, have the confidence to have the child and stand up for her entitlement to be a mother – and a mother of a mixed-race child.

One thinks of Marilyn Monroe who was said to have had 12 abortions during her fertile life: it is established that she certainly had several. It may be said that a woman who has 12 abortions is not taking care of herself and there may have been an underlying self-destructive reason for this behaviour. However, in the climate of the time, Monroe would also have lost her position as a glamorous sex symbol if she had given birth to a child, particularly if out of wedlock. Today, a baby is a glittering trophy for any movie star or celebrity, not a handicap. No doubt film actresses have abortions when it suits them, but it is evident that they feel more confident about choosing motherhood too, since so many of the screen stars are mothers, and will adopt babies if they cannot conceive.

Women seem also less easily pressed into abortion by rich or influential men than was formerly the case. Several examples come to my mind, in the early 1960s, where a woman felt obliged to have an abortion because the man insisted that she ought to. Men would plead, cajole and sometimes try to bribe a woman to terminate an inconvenient pregnancy: and it worked. A well-known television celebrity in the 1960s successfully persuaded a young woman who was pregnant by him to go to Switzerland for an abortion, the better to combine the operation with a luxurious holiday.

This is now distinctly *mal vu*. It has been suggested that Cecil Parkinson tried to press his mistress Sarah Keays into an abortion in 1983 and the media, reacting in January 2002, condemned this as the act of a bounder. (On a point of information, I received a letter from Lord Parkinson in the mid-1980s – when I wrote to him to elicit his views on the subject – saying that he would NEVER suggest an abortion to a woman, as he considered it to be wrong.) Consider, too, the case of the actress and model Liz Hurley, who was proud to announce her pregnancy in 2001. In an interview with William Cash in *The Sunday Telegraph* on 11 November 2001 it is made quite clear that Ms Hurley's lover, Mr Steve Bing, indicated that he expected her to have an abortion, since the pregnancy did not suit him. In an interview published in the *Mail on Sunday* on 9 December 2001, one of Mr Bing's supporters said he thought Ms Hurley was on the Pill, and that he made it clear he did not wish to take any responsibility for the pregnancy.

From this moment on, Steve Bing became (with some justification) characterized in the tabloid media as a 'love rat' and the notion that he would press for an abortion was regarded as quite revolting. It is significant that nowadays a showgirl like Liz Hurley has the confidence to continue in a pregnancy and is in no danger of being intimidated by a rich man into an abortion. Contrast this with the case of Joseph Kennedy, the rich and cynical (and publicly Catholic) father of President John F. Kennedy: when he made the actress Gloria Swanson pregnant in the 1930s he insisted she have an abortion and, forever after regretting it, she acceded to his command.

Thus, legal and easily accessible abortion has had some interesting outcomes: the language of choice has penetrated many other areas of people's lives. Opponents of abortion have moved vigorously and constructively to support women in connected areas of fertility and motherhood – the pro-life organizations in Britain now have a network of supporting Asian girls who might otherwise be punished by their families, married off or coerced into an abortion for the sake of respectability. Paradoxically, the impact of abortion rights has, in some instances, been to enhance the 'pro-life' position. This can be seen in the use of language and the discourse in popular media over the past 35 years.

CHANGING LANGUAGE

After abortion became legal, language surrounding abortion rights was hard-edged and aggressive. It was a point of honour to speak about 'the fetus', because that de-personalized the issue, and 'baby' was considered 'loaded'. (An abortion agency counsellor told me that any woman who uses the word baby when pregnant, is 'in trouble' – that is, she probably does not really want an abortion.) In the 1970s, feminism was anti-baby and anti-family. When British *Cosmopolitan* was launched in 1972, the editor promised that the word baby would never be mentioned, 'except in the context of abortion'. There were, it is true, continuing attempts to repeal or to curb the 1967 Act, and feminists and pro-choice liberals felt they had to be tough in defending abortion rights. The admired feminist icons – Germaine Greer, Gloira Steinem, Kate Millett, and *Cosmopolitan* founder Helen Gurley Brown, a feminist in her own, rather commercial, way – were childless.

However, once abortion rights were legally secured, the focus in the sphere of reproduction switched to fertility. The hot topic, after the birth of Louise Brown in 1978, was assisted fertility. I saw doctors whom I knew were practised abortion operators re-brand themselves as 'fertility experts'. Embryology and fetology developed as new sciences. We learned more and more about the development of the unborn: science is, in some respects, 'pro-life' because it tends to agree that clinically life does indeed begin at conception, or at the very least, at fertilization. Abortion liberals who had once dismissed the embryo (the unborn at under eight weeks pregnancy) as 'an undifferentiated clump of cells' turned out to be biologically wrong and pro-life conservatives who insisted that the unborn was a unique individual from the start were endorsed by all the advances of DNA.

As medical science advanced on one plane popular approval, even sentimentality, towards the baby went on apace on the other. We have become much more aware of the value of the baby, whether born or unborn, and two recent examples again illustrate this. When the Countess of Wessex had an ectopic pregnancy diagnosed in early December 2001, she was six weeks pregnant. Six weeks is very early in a pregnancy and the embryo would be very small indeed, although nevertheless a tiny human. The tabloid press immediately responded with banner headlines: 'Sophie loses baby' and followed the story with tragic descriptions of 'the secret baby' which Prince Edward and his wife were already cherishing. 'Countess and Edward sad and shaken by their loss', wrote *The Sun* on 7 December. All of the press reported the 'baby loss' as a major story, and none of the popular press used the word 'embryo'.

In the second very touching case of Gordon and Sarah Brown, whose premature baby became ill and died, there was an outpouring of grief with huge banner headlines across the front page of the *Daily Telegraph*. There was immense sadness for the Browns, and I was commissioned to write a commentary piece. In my postbag I received letters from women who, recalling similar circumstances 40 and 50 years previously, described how little attention was paid to their dead premature child. It was as though a premature baby, then, hardly counted. In our time both miscarriage and the death of a premature baby are, rightly, considered a loss and a grief. The unborn child and the premature baby have been personalized by popular culture. Unconsciously, the tabloids recognize that even a very early embryo is a 'baby'; just as popular culture so aptly nicknamed In Vitro Fertilization 'test-tube baby'. Television (and even sometimes *The Guardian*) usually prefers the word 'unborn' to 'fetus': a famous doctor of fetal medicine is described as the wonderful physician 'who treats the unborn'. Every advance which recognizes that the child conceived in the womb is a human being endorses, at some level, the right to life.

CONCLUSION

So whose right on abortion? It was always a matter of conflicting rights – the right to choose against the right to life. In some respects, an uneasy truce has now settled over the issue. Pro-choice advocates have won the legal battles in most advanced countries – a few, such as Ireland and Portugal, still holding out. But pro-life holds the moral and popular-culture high ground, and has been assisted by the newly developing fetal sciences. People may accept that women have abortions, but it seldom confers esteem. The woman who proceeds with a pregnancy in the most difficult circumstances is admired as a Mother Courage whereas the woman who opts for an abortion in easy circumstances may be said to be exercising 'her right to choose' – yet would seldom command esteem. There are no greetings cards for 'Congrats! You've just had a lovely abortion!' The word abortion has retained its connection with failure, with ugliness, even with something disgusting: a building described as 'an abortion of architecture' is understood as a blight on the landscape.

Opinion polls tend to show that people accept that abortion should be legal, but it does not follow that they always consider it moral. It is now more widely conceded that it is a woman's right to choose what she does with her body; at the same time, it is more deeply recognized that the body within her body is a small human one, and that, as it grows, it acquires more rights. The ambivalence of the rights issue was eloquently expressed by a woman who said to me, remembering her abortion decision: 'It was the right thing to do at the time, but it's wrong just the same.' Rights in themselves do not always provide a sufficiently wide moral vocabulary for this complex issue.

Perspectives on abortion have changed over the past 35 years and will change again in the coming times. It is being predicted that within a generation 'there will probably be mass use of artificial wombs to grow babies', according to Jeremy Rifkin, author of *The Biotech Century* (2001). Dr Hung Chiung Liu of the Centre for Reproductive Medicine and Fertility at Cornell University is making great strides towards the artificial womb, which could house and grown the unborn child. When 'the right to choose' is extended to the further choice of destroying the unborn or, alternatively, donating it to grow in a synthetic womb, then we will surely be in a whole new moral dilemma once more.

AFTERWORD
Ellie Lee

Abortion is a moral problem. The existence of a moral problem presupposes some conflict of values or goals or interests. A solution to a moral problem is a resolution of such conflict; the purpose of moral principles is to tell us how to resolve the moral conflicts.

What is at stake for the fetus is life itself... What is at stake for the woman is autonomy – control of the use to be made of her body.

L.W. Sumner

In 1981, the North American philosopher L. W. Sumner summarized the issue at the centre of the debate about abortion this way in his book *Abortion and Moral Theory*. For Sumner, the question 'Abortion: Whose Right?' raises the matter of competing moralities. How it is answered depends on whether respect for the bodily autonomy of the pregnant woman – her right to decide whether to continue or end a pregnancy – is considered more or less valuable and important for society than respect for the life of the fetus. The essays in this book have discussed three main dimensions of this issue.

◆●●
●　●
●●◆ **MORALITY AND LAW**

One issue that has been addressed is the implications that different ways of resolving the moral problem of abortion have for the law. The resolution of this issue in favour of the interests of the fetus has been advocated, which would mean that abortion would be made illegal. Abortion would be treated as homicide.

This approach would, of course, raise the issue of what should happen to those women who attempt to terminate pregnancies. It was indeed this issue that led in part to the pressure to introduce the 1967 Abortion Act in the first place. The status of abortion as an illegal act did not prevent thousands of women attempting to end pregnancies. Yet there was little will to prosecute either them or those who assisted them. This disparity between the widespread practice of illegal abortion, and its criminalized status, generated the impulse towards legal reform and those who advocate that abortion should be treated legally as murder might justifiably be questioned about the practical consequences of their argument.

Its resolution in favour of respect for bodily autonomy has also been argued for. This would imply certainly that the current law in Britain, through which abortion is criminalized but can legally be performed where doctors deem in necessary, would be replaced. The form of law presented by some arguments in this book as preferable would extract regulation of access to abortion from the realm of the law altogether. There would be no special law to regulate access to abortion. Rather, requests from women for abortion would be considered *prima facie* acceptable.

This argument draws on the notion that in a civilized society, moral authority should be ceded to individuals when decisions are to be made about their reproductive lives. No one other than the individual concerned, in this case the pregnant woman, should have the right, or responsibility, to decide how to pursue their reproductive lives. While others, most importantly doctors, should play an important role in deciding what is for the best in clinical decisions, in abortion, where the key considerations shaping the decision a woman make are not *clinical* but are profoundly personal, deciding what is for the best is a matter for the pregnant woman herself.

By some who argue for reform of the law in this direction, it is considered positive and important that medical law has, in general, come to place a great deal of importance on the concept of 'patient autonomy' and the rights of patients to make decisions about their treatment. Decisions about abortion, it is suggested, should be included in, not exempted from, this general trajectory of medical law. Women's right to make decisions about their medical treatment in abortion should be considered no differently from the right of patients to do so in general, in other areas of medicine.

Some arguments in this book suggest, however, that those who advocate this kind of approach to reform of the abortion law need to consider carefully the implications of their case for arguments about the role of the doctor. Is the notion of 'patient autonomy' beneficial to the practice of medicine where decisions about abortion are to be made?

MORALITY AND THE ROLE OF THE DOCTOR

One point of consensus that emerges from the essays in this book is that while formally under British law doctors would authorize requests for abortion only on fairly limited medical grounds, in practice, in the early stages of pregnancy at least, abortion is available at the request of the pregnant woman. Doctors are now, in general, unlikely to make it difficult for women to access abortion, and doctors' organizations have encouraged this development. Contesting opinions have been expressed about whether this approach is positive or negative.

On the one hand, this development has been considered to be part of the ethos that has come to strongly influence medical practice, which elevates the importance of 'patient rights'. The argument has been made that it is negative for both doctors and patients in general that the 'rights' of the patient have come to be considered so important in guiding the doctor–patient relationship. With regard to abortion in particular, it has been argued that this approach has 'demoralized' the practice of medicine, and means that doctors are no longer taking on their responsibility of encouraging patients to think about the morality of their actions. From this perspective, it would be preferable if the spirit that underpinned the reform of the abortion law in 1967 was revived. Doctors should consider abortion to be morally wrong in general, but acceptable in certain circumstances, and should ensure that the law is enacted in this spirit.

In contrast no one, it is argued, including a doctor, is better positioned than the woman herself to decide whether abortion is the best course of action to take. Abortion cannot be thought of as directly comparable to many other medical procedures, in that the main question that the pregnant woman has to resolve is not a clinical one. Whether she has an abortion, or continues the pregnancy, both outcomes in regard of her health are pretty safe, and what is really at issue is whether in her own situation, the woman considers it best to end or continue the pregnancy. From this perspective, not only is it positive that doctors are less likely to place barriers in the way than in the past when a woman states she wants to end a pregnancy, but legal reform to clarify that the woman is at the centre of the decision would benefit both doctors and women. It would reflect accurately who is in the best position to decide about the outcome of a pregnancy, and mean that neither doctors nor women had to misrepresent their views, as they may have to under the current legal framework.

This is not to say that the interaction between the pregnant woman and the doctor should inevitably come to rest on a technicality – where the doctor simply arranges, or performs an abortion with no meaningful conversation or exchange with his or her patient. To the contrary, such interaction is likely to be *more* meaningful where recognition is given legally to the idea that the woman has a right to make this decision. In this situation, the doctor–patient relationship would not be muddied by concern on the part of the woman that the doctor may refuse her request, and instead a more honest exchange about the issues of concern for the woman could take place.

Given the pivotal role of the doctor in abortion, in any circumstance where abortion is legal, the matter of how to best think about the kind of relationship between pregnant woman and medical practitioners that works well for both parties is a key question in the abortion debate.

MORALITY, WOMEN'S LIVES AND THE ABORTION DEBATE

A third part of the picture that has been discussed in the essays in this book is the relationship between abortion and the ideas that are discussed in the debate about it, and broader changes in women's lives. The discourse on abortion, it has been argued, has shifted significantly in the past 30 years. Why and how abortion is discussed has changed as women's lives and, in particular, the place of motherhood in them, has altered.

It has been argued that the idea that women should be able to make choices in their reproductive lives has come to pervade thinking across the board. The idea of choice, first articulated in relation to abortion to express the notion that women should not always have to continue pregnancies and that motherhood should be optional not compulsory, has become highly influential and has shaped many debates. Interestingly, it has been argued, this idea has enabled women to more easily decide to *continue* pregnancies, as well as end them. The idea of choice has not only undermined the notion that abortion is always morally wrong, but has also legitimized other kinds of reproductive decisions. For those who oppose abortion morally, the idea of choice has not proved entirely negative in this regard.

It has also been argued, perhaps in contrast, that social change since 1967 has acted to undermine and marginalize anti-abortion opinion to a significant degree. Women now expect and are expected to engage with the public world of work and education, not only that of home and family, 'planned parenthood' has become accepted as desirable, and delaying or opting out of having children altogether are commonplace for women. Such change in women's lives has been accepted, if not embraced, by most and with it abortion has become a fact of life. In this context, it has been argued, those who oppose abortion in principle have a very limited audience, even amongst social conservatives. The real question, therefore, is not so much whether abortion should be legal or not legal, but whether it will be 'de-stigmatized' and come to be accepted in law and policy as a morally legitimate choice for women.

While it seems unlikely that abortion will at the present time become the subject of high profile debate among politicians in Britain, we hope the essays in this book will help encourage debate in other arenas about an issue which raises important questions about the role of morality and law in reflecting and shaping social developments.

DEBATING MATTERS

Institute of Ideas
Expanding the Boundaries of Public Debate

If you have found this book interesting,
and agree that 'debating matters', you can
find out more about the Institute of Ideas
and our programme of live conferences and
debates by visiting our website
www.instituteofideas.com.
Alternatively you can email
info@instituteofideas.com
or call 020 7269 9220 to receive a full
programme of events and information about
joining the Institute of Ideas.

Other titles available in this series:

DEBATING MATTERS

Institute of Ideas
Expanding the Boundaries of Public Debate

ANIMAL EXPERIMENTATION:

GOOD OR BAD?

Some argue that animal experiments are vital to advance scientific knowledge and improve medical practice. Others believe that they are unnecessary, cruel and repetitive. Do animals experience pain and suffering in the same ways as humans; if so should they be given rights? Is a compromise between animal rights campaigners and those who emphasize the needs of humans possible or even desirable?

Key figures in the debate exchange their views on this contentious issue:

- Dr Stuart Derbyshire, scientist at the University of Pittsburgh, US, researching central mechanisms of pain
- Dr Mark Matfield, medical research scientist
- Dr Tom Regan, Professor of Philosophy and President of The Culture & Animals Foundation
- Dr Richard D. Ryder, author of *Painism: a Modern Morality*.

ETHICAL TOURISM:

WHO BENEFITS?

The idea of 'responsible tourism' has grown in popularity over the past decade. But who benefits from this notion? Should the behaviour of travellers come under scrutiny? What are the consequences of this new etiquette for the travelling experience? Can we make a positive difference if we change the way the travel?

Contrasting responses to these questions come from:

- Dea Birkett, columnist for *The Guardian* and author of *Amazonian*
- Jim Butcher, Senior Lecturer, Department of Geography and Tourism, Canterbury Christ Church University College
- Paul Goldstein, Marketing Manager, Exodus Travel
- Dr Harold Goodwin, Director of the Centre for Responsible Tourism at the University of Greenwich
- Kirk Leech, Assistant Director of the youth charity Worldwrite

REALITY TV:

HOW REAL IS REAL?

What is reality TV, and how real is it anyway? From gameshows such as *Big Brother* to docusoaps and even history programmes, television seems to be turning its attentions onto 'real people'. Does this mean that television is becoming more democratic, or is reality TV a fad that has had its day? Does reality TV reflect society as it really is, or merely manufacture disposable celebrities?

Contrasting views come from:

- Christopher Dunkley, television critic for the *Financial Times*
- Dr Graham Barnfield, Lecturer in Journalism,
  The Surrey Institute of Art & Design
- Victoria Mapplebeck, TV producer of the TV shows
  Smart Hearts and *Meet the Kilshaws*
- Bernard Clark, documentary maker.

TEENAGE SEX:

WHAT SHOULD SCHOOLS TEACH CHILDREN?

Under New Labour, sex education is a big priority. New policies in this area are guaranteed to generate a furious debate. 'Pro-family' groups contend that young people are not given a clear message about right and wrong. Others argue there is still too little sex education. And some worry that all too often sex education stigmatizes sex. So what should schools teach children about sex?

Contrasting approaches to this topical and contentious question are debated by:

- Simon Blake, Director of the Sex Education Forum
- Peter Hitchens, a columnist for the *Mail on Sunday*
- Janine Jolly, health promotion specialist
- David J. Landry, of the US based Alan Guttmacher Institute
- Peter Tatchell, human rights activist
- Stuart Waiton, journalist and researcher.

DESIGNER BABIES:

WHERE SHOULD WE DRAW THE LINE?

Science fiction has been preoccupied with technologies to control the characteristics of our children since the publication of Aldous Huxley's *Brave New World*. Current arguments about 'designer babies' almost always demand that lines should be drawn and regulations tightened. But where should regulation stop and patient choice in the use of reproductive technology begin?

The following contributors set out their arguments:

- Juliet Tizzard, advocate for advances in reproductive medicine
- Professor John Harris, ethicist
- Veronica English and Ann Sommerville of the British Medical Association
- Josephine Quintavalle, pro-life spokesperson
- Agnes Fletcher, disability rights campaigner.

COMPENSATION CRAZY:

DO WE BLAME AND CLAIM TOO MUCH?

Big compensation pay-outs make the headlines. New style 'claims centres' advertise for accident victims promising 'where there's blame, there's a claim'. Many commentators fear Britain is experiencing a US-style compensation craze. But what's wrong with holding employers and businesses to account? Or are we now too ready to reach for our lawyers and to find someone to blame when things go wrong?

These questions and more are discussed by:

- Ian Walker, personal injury litigator
- Tracey Brown, risk analyst
- John Peysner, Professor of civil litigation
- Daniel Lloyd, lawyer.

ALTERNATIVE MEDICINE:

SHOULD WE SWALLOW IT?

Complementary and Alternative Medicine (CAM) is an increasingly acceptable part of the repertory of healthcare professionals and is becoming more and more popular with the public. It seems that CAM has come of age – but should we swallow it?

Contributors to this book make the case for and against CAM:

- Michael Fitzpatrick, General Practitioner and author of *The Tyranny of Health*
- Brid Hehir, nurse and regular contributor to the nursing press
- Sarah Cant, Senior Lecturer in Applied Social Sciences
- Anthony Campbell, Emeritus Consultant Physician at The Royal London Homeopathic Hospital
- Michael Fox, Chief Executive of the Foundation for Integrated Medicine.